W9-BVC-338

George Norris, Going Home

Reflections of a Progressive Statesman

GENE A. BUDIG AND DON WALTON

Preface by George W. Norris

University of Nebraska Press | Lincoln and London

∞

Library of Congress Cataloging-in-Publication Data

Budig, Gene A., author.

George Norris, going home: reflections of a progressive statesman /
Gene A. Budig and Don Walton ; preface by George W. Norris.

pages cm

ISBN 978-0-8032-7187-6 (pbk.: alk. paper) 1. Norris, George W.
(George William), 1861-1944. 2. United States. Congress. Senate—
Biography. 3. Legislators—United States—Biography. 4. Legislators—
Nebraska—Biography. 5. Nebraska—Biography. I. Walton, Don (Don
Brooks), author. II. Title.

E748.N65B83 2013

328.73′092—dc23   [B]   2013018806

Set in Lyon by Laura Wellington.

Designed by J. Vadnais.

Contents

Illustrations

Preface

Defeat was a word George W. Norris seldom used, even after his people rejected him at the polls in 1942. Few Nebraskans realized the impact of their decision upon the senior senator from McCook.

From his rocking chair in his Southwest Nebraska home, Norris exposed his broken heart for the first and only time.

I wrote this on Thursday, before Christmas, and regarded it as complete, but the next day, being the day before Christmas, I listened to the President of the United States make his famous speech over the radio to our armies fighting in various battle fronts all over the world. I was completely overcome by the eloquence of the President's address. In this address the President said that within the next two or three weeks he expected to deliver an official message to Congress, in which he expected to go into more details about the things he had to say about the conferences that had taken place in Cairo and Teheran with Churchill, Chiang Kai-shek, and Josef Stalin.

Like a dream it seemed to me I was sitting again in the capital of the United States, listening to the voice I knew so well, eloquently detailing his report of those conferences. Surrounded by my senatorial associates, I could hear again so plainly that analysis of the international situation, and in my dream, for dream it was, I applauded the sentiments that had carried me into dreamland, and by my own applause I was awakened and it dawned upon me like a flash piercing my very heart that I was no longer a member of the Senate, listening to the President's eloquent voice, but that after all, I was just a private citizen, sitting in my home at McCook, Nebraska. I realized then that I would not be present when that official message was delivered, that my own people whom I loved and whom I had tried to serve for the major part of my adult life had made it impossible for me to longer represent them in the capital of the United States, and as I passed from dreamland into reality, I likened myself to the private soldier who had fought during the entire war, and that just as victory had come to our embattled soldiers, and just as the rising sun of civilization was shedding its sunlight of human liberty over the mountains, across the sea and through the jungles, when the struggle was all over, when the war had been won and the last charge that had brought victory, he fell, pierced by an enemy bullet, and slowly sank into an honored but unknown grave.

McCook, Nebraska
G. W. Norris
December 24, 1943

Introduction

This project began nearly fifty-three years ago when two young newspaper reporters from the *Lincoln Star* became intrigued by the remarkable achievements of George W. Norris, the United States Senator from Nebraska who, among other great accomplishments, fathered the Tennessee Valley Authority Act and the Rural Electrification Act for the federal government, and the Unicameral legislature for the state of Nebraska.

Much of this book was the product of lengthy interviews with Ellie Norris, the political legend's wife. She gave freely of her time and insight during conversations at the Norris home in McCook, Nebraska, which is listed on the National Register of Historic Places. The conversational narrative and thoughts attributed to Norris, along with the detailed scene setting, are based on Mrs. Norris's recollections and memory. This is a story largely told through her eyes.

Mrs. Norris described the senator as a complex human being and steadfast public figure with a far-reaching impact on national and international events. She saw George William, as she called him, as an inspirational leader who counted members of the Congress and the President of the United States as colleagues and friends.

Norris was unbending when it came to doing what he thought

was right. He always saw his role in elective politics as one based on trust, believing that the people of the Cornhusker State chose him to vote his conscience. He knew that he would be the target of intense criticism from time to time. But he also knew that he must remain true to his convictions. He never relied on polls.

Norris was born in 1861 on a farm in Sandusky County, Ohio, the eleventh child of poor, uneducated farmers of Scots-Irish and Pennsylvania Dutch descent. He graduated from Baldwin University and earned his bachelor of laws degree in 1883 at the Law School of Valparaiso University in Indiana.

He moved to McCook in 1900 where he became engaged in the law and Republican politics. As a steel-willed young congressman, Norris led the revolt against Speaker Joseph G. Cannon in 1910. By a vote of 191 to 156, the House created a new system that took autocratic power away from the speaker and replaced it with a system of seniority that automatically moved members ahead, even against the wishes of leadership.

Later, Senator Norris was a staunch supporter of President Franklin Roosevelt's New Deal programs, particularly the Tennessee Valley Authority. The TVA is still the nation's largest public power provider, founded to address a wider range of environmental, economic, and technological issues, including the delivery of low-cost electricity and the management of natural resources. Its service territory includes most of Tennessee and parts of Alabama, Georgia, Kentucky, Mississippi, North Carolina, and Virginia. Norris was such a committed supporter of the TVA that the massive dam built for the project was named in his honor, as was a city in Tennessee.

The man from Nebraska was the prime Senate mover behind the Rural Electrification Act, which brought electrification service to underserved and unserved rural areas across the United States. Norris lit the countrysides, which enhanced the quality of life immeasurably. He always believed in "public power," and today Nebraska remains wholly served by public energy. The REA grew to represent over nine hundred electric cooperatives in forty-seven states and ultimately served 12 percent of the population across the country.

Many of his usually conservative followers were apprehensive about the direction of the Roosevelt presidency, but in the end they generally lined up behind the senator. Norris never forgot that act of faith in his vision, and he mentioned it often when in Nebraska. The New Deal, he thought, was essential if America was to survive and move toward full recovery.

Norris also believed in the wisdom of common people and power of new ideas. "To get good government and to retain it, it is necessary that a liberty-loving, educated, intelligent people should be ever watchful, to carefully guard and protect their rights and liberties," he said in 1934 while campaigning for creation of a single-house, nonpartisan legislature in Nebraska.

State Senator Richard Marvel of Hastings, longtime chairman of the Unicameral Budget Committee, observed that the Nebraska Legislature "did much to keep everyone in line—legislators and lobbyists. It provided a transparent form of government."

No other state followed suit, but most applauded its concept. Legislators outside Nebraska were reluctant to vote themselves out of office; it was that simple, according to Governor John Connally of Texas, who invited his gubernatorial counterpart from Nebraska, Frank B. Morrison, to address the two-house legislature in the Lone Star state.

Norris also dared to oppose President Roosevelt's Judiciary Reorganization Plan of 1937 to pack the Supreme Court, and he often railed against corrupt patronage.

The great senator's work was widely recognized in his day. When the Senate established a special committee in 1955 to select five outstanding former members whose portraits would be permanently displayed in the Senate Reception Room, it turned to 160 American historians and biographers for recommendations. More of those scholars recommended Norris than any other senator.

He was one of eight senators featured in John F. Kennedy's Pulitzer Prize–winning book, *Profiles in Courage*, for opposing Speaker Cannon's autocratic power in the House, for speaking out against arming U.S. merchant ships during the United States' period of neutrality preceding its entrance to World War I, and for supporting the presidential campaign of Democrat Al Smith of New York, who just happened to be Catholic.

Theodore C. Sorensen, the renowned speechwriter and political advisor to President Kennedy, who helped write *Profiles in Courage*, told two reporters from Lincoln that George W. Norris made him proud of his Nebraska heritage.

So much can be said about the historic professional achievements of Norris, but Ellie Norris also brought keen insights to who he was as a man. In so many ways, this is her book. It is part of her tribute to her husband, whom she saw as a "broken man" after being turned out by the Nebraska electorate.

The interviews with Mrs. Norris, along with accompanying research, resulted in a series of articles for the Lincoln morning newspaper and the Associated Press. The writers were pleased with the readership and hoped to someday publish a book on George W. Norris, but those plans never materialized.

The writers took different professional paths. But they kept in contact and from time to time, talked about their resolve to bring closure to the Norris matter. It was Gretchen Budig, wife of one of those two once-young men, who found the manuscript, yellowed by time, in the corner of an attic. She read it and was struck by its relevance; she found it to be a moving story about an American hero and pushed the two authors to complete the literary venture with publication in a book.

The authors thought it time to remind the people of Nebraska and the Midwest, and all others, especially the younger ones, of the remarkable role George Norris played in the history of the nation and his state.

George Norris, Going Home

One

The clackety-clack of steel against steel jarred him.

He was slumped in the overstuffed comfort of a two-room compartment speeding west across the valleys of the East. The rails led toward home, but first to St. Louis, where he would be toasted tenderly in the Mississippi Valley. He was tired—but they were kind enough to ask him to stop, and he would.

Peering into the dark, George William Norris could spot fringes of winter clumped along the tracks. It was January. And it was cold, he thought, perhaps colder than any winter month he could remember. The wind was bitter and the warm comfort of the train soothed him. The sudden jerk that signaled the beginning of a long journey halfway across the continent had jolted him.

Now the rhythmic clatter of cold steel pounded at his senses, and Norris began to realize once again that it was really true. Was this the beginning of a journey or the end?

The trip to the station at Silver Spring had been quiet. Jack Robertson, his loyal son-in-law and, as Norris often said, the most proficient secretary on the Hill, had driven him down in the 1937 Buick. Daughter Hazel had come with him. And, of course, Ellie.

Leaving the lovely garden at the Dodge Hotel had not been easy—but then, nothing would be easy from now on. It had been a painful two months, and much sorrow lay ahead, Norris quietly assured himself.

It was a little difficult to comprehend. No more would he walk the streets of Washington; no more would he be privileged to rise on the floor of the Senate to voice his indignation against those he believed would surely sap the nation's strength and sack its resources if a voice were not raised.

Now, he was stripped of the power to battle for what he believed. Yes, he could still talk. He could shout and cry out—but would they hear his voice a thousand miles away? Oh, there were others in the Senate who could speak for the people, others to stand guard over the public's property. But Norris had been doing it for so long that he had already made his enemies, and perhaps it was easier for him to speak without the hesitation that might confront another. He'd been doing it for forty years, the last three decades as a member of the Senate. In the Senate, they had to listen to you. It's too easy to ignore a private citizen, especially if he is one who has been rejected by his own people. That is what hurt.

George Norris felt no bitterness. Only pain—and it gnawed at his vitality, robbed him of his strength, burned like a hot coal or steel in the sun. He had resolved never to speak of it. He would live with it, accept it as an unwelcome but constant companion that would walk with him, talk to him, eat with him, sleep with him the rest of his days.

He would never try to explain why he lost. There were plenty of political reasons that he would hear again and again. He had entered the 1942 Senate race too late. He had campaigned too little. He had vacillated too long during the long summer months that had led to his decision, and he had lost the support of friends who in the meantime had committed themselves to Ken Wherry.

He was the victim of an anti-Roosevelt vote that had swept the vast flat spaces of his beloved state. The nation was at war, and perhaps Nebraskans were disappointed at the performance of his friend in the White House. Norris was eighty-one, and that may have cost him votes. But all these political considerations did not matter.

George Norris would never try to evaluate the meaning of this defeat for one reason: he was deathly afraid. He feared what it might mean. He shuddered to think of it. The voice of the people had been raised against all that Norris stood for, against all that he had labored for and battled and endured. That's what he feared: all the progress that had been hammered out through the sweat and tears of forty years of social struggle might go by the board. Were the people ready to toss away progress, turn their backs on it just when it needed them most? Were the benefits of the Rural Electrification Administration to be overlooked, and its strength bartered away in the houses of Congress? And was the Tennessee Valley Authority—a creature of George Norris that had died a thousand deaths on its long road to reality—to be suddenly ignored, allowed to slip into degeneration and ruin?

Perhaps, Norris gloomed, the end had come for such dreams. Even if they were allowed to continue, the lesson learned from their service would surely be discarded. There would be no more TVA's, no more public control of the vast resources of the land if the people had voted against the TVA when they rejected Norris. All of it stood in mortal danger of dropping by the wayside, falling into the ruins of the past. It might be ignored when it needed nurture, a weak and growing child who demanded new strength if it were to survive. Ah, that's what hurt—was the end now in sight for it all?

Steadily, the train rolled west, leaving farther behind in darkness many of the things that had made Washington home for Norris.

There was the big green Buick that faithfully served him on

daily trips to and from the Senate chambers and on long Sunday afternoon excursions through the country. It symbolized the life of Norris—one of motion.

Even on that cold January night, the oversized 1937 sedan glistened farewell. Its gleam flashed back memories of many a long and tedious car-polishing session with Norris attentively supervising.

Ellie knew that the car had meant much to George William, as it had to the rest of the Norris brood. It became a member of the family, meriting continual respect and care. That was why Norris found it hard to understand Ellie's apparent lack of concern in getting it to McCook as soon as possible. His frequent suggestions for possible transportation for the Buick drew a quick shifting of subject by Ellie. Much as it hurt her, Ellie realized that George William's days behind the wheel were over. The car would stay with Hazel and Jack in Washington, and Ellie would be taxed to think of new reasons for the delay in shipment. But convincing reasons grew hard and Norris grew impatient.

Only Ellie knew that George William's shattered heart and searching eyes grew weaker by the day. And what was she to do but wait at his side, pray, and try to understand the hand of God?

The Buick symbolized many pleasant memories. Norris could remember well the day he purchased the shiny green machine. They had gone to Woodbridge, Virginia, to procure the car from a dealer who had long wanted to sell him an auto. Since then it had shared his journeys, traveled the streets of the capital with him, and housed many a famous passenger and those he dearly loved. Norris wanted very much to take the car back home this time. But Norris's old cronies along B Street in McCook were never to see or ride in the big Buick that George William had so often referred to with a sense of pride. Nor were they to see many of the other belongings that he often spoke of and held sacred.

The roughly bound set of law books he had used as district judge at McCook, the pen FDR had given him after signing the TVA into being, and the crudely penciled letter from the Kansas farm wife who beseeched his continued support of the REA—all were to remain behind in Washington.

And only the good Lord knew how much George William wanted these at his fingertips at the end. Though slight in monetary value, these odds and ends symbolized priceless achievement and tearful disappointment.

But the delegation of close friends and associates begged him to leave them behind. Loud and often, they told him that he owed it to posterity; that he owed it to other young men seeking to follow his footsteps in government; and that he owed it to Nebraska and his country. They flattered with words of a possible national shrine and lasting international recognition. Norris listened politely as he had throughout his career on the Hill; only this time he remained silent. Finally he nodded; they sighed; and Ellie saw another blow to his already strained heart.

True, the belongings remained and are still on display, but the vivid memories went home with the tired old gentleman from Nebraska. He knew that he could never forget the many hours spent over the crinkled, yellow law texts; the quick wink and sincere handshake of FDR; the almost pathetic words of hope from the Kansas farm wife. These and hundreds of other recollections chaperoned him to the end.

The wintry winds gently tapped on George William's compartment door as the massive coal-fed giant sped on westward. Except for the light rap and clicking flashlight of the tireless conductor, George William and Ellie sat alone in a voiceless world. Their thoughts now were on the future.

Broken, crushed, and tossed into the rubbish of defeat were his golden plans for tomorrow. The TVA, he believed, could be just a beginning. The Missouri, the Mississippi, and all the nation's major channels could be harnessed in the same manner. Flood control, navigational aid, and public power could be provided to all the people at low cost. Great dams would be erected to hold the water's surge; vast power plants would arise to light the land; the water would be controlled, and fields would flourish.

Why not develop all of America's rivers in the same manner that had brought prosperity to the Tennessee Valley? Of course, it would be a real battle. The opposition was ready, strong, firm, adamant. But had not the TVA itself been a long and weary war? It had proved itself, and now (or as soon as the war came to an end) was the time to expand it to other valleys. Norris had anticipated the struggle with zeal. Now his banner was gone. He could not lead the charge—and who else would? A cloud of woe settled over the dejected traveler.

Washington had been one long adventure for Norris. He had counseled with presidents, debated all the major issues of these turbulent times with his colleagues in the Senate, and fought the trusts. It had been an arduous task, but it had also been exhilarating. A crusade, a mission, a sense of devotion to duty had nourished Norris and kept him hard at the stern.

He would miss the man in the White House. That visionary giant, Norris thought, that devoted humanitarian. They had shared lunch together many times on trays in the President's office and discussed one broad topic—the world. The President confided in him, unfolded his dreams before him, spoke of politics, strategy, and the distant future now shrouded in the fog of war.

Roosevelt could be kind, Norris knew. But he could also be hard, firm, resolute, unbending, unyielding, even harsh. The President won his battles because he believed in them enough to pour all the resources at his command into the struggle. The greatest of these weapons was the people.

They had responded to Norris too—in five campaigns for a seat in the House and five bitter Senate struggles. Now, they had turned a deaf ear, shown him their backs, denied him their confidence, wheeled and walked away. Was this also to happen to Roosevelt? This too worried George Norris, for it was FDR who had finally pushed the TVA off dead center and given it life. It was Roosevelt who had turned the switch that brought REA electricity to the farms of the nation. It was the President who had launched the republic on the road to social justice.

If Roosevelt were to be turned down in 1944, Norris thought, this would be the end of it all. The barons of private exploitation would return to their thrones. The public's property would be divided and distributed, hacked to pieces, taken from the people. Norris could endure his defeat, but he could not bear to think of the hazardous future that might lie ahead for his nation.

In Washington that cold January night, Roosevelt too wondered what the election in Nebraska might mean.

Regularly, the senator's furrowed brow would fall, leaving his pronounced chin buried in the crease of his freshly starched white shirt. He dozed, gasping breaths of uneasy air. Ellie watched and hoped that the night's weight would remain on his heavy eyelids until the train screeched to a halt in St. Louis. Her hopes went for naught. The conductor's nagging cough, the leaking water fountain, and the hungry infant down the corridor all keyed George William's shifting of positions. He would open his eyes, look around, and then drop back into mental seclusion.

Never had Ellie felt more compassion for a human being than she did for George William. But how could she help? It was done—his people had answered his desire to serve again with a thoughtless nay. The wound had been inflicted, the damage done.

Two

At the gloomy, time-scarred old station, a delegation of officials and friends waited. They chatted about the weather, flipped through the morning newspapers, and sipped at hot coffee in the noisy lunchroom. The dank old building echoed with the steps of weary travelers, many of whose trains had been delayed by the snow.

Outside, trainsmen were at work along the platform. Kids ran up and down the long slab, seemingly for no reason at all. Baggage was segregated in small clumps along the trackside. A vendor busily peddled the morning edition.

In the lunchroom, newsmen gulped black coffee and identified some of the waiting dignitaries. They agreed on the general line of questioning that would be pursued at the press conference later in the morning. It was decided that the significance of his defeat would be thoroughly explored. Comments on late national news contained in the morning dispatches would also be sought. News photographers were briefed on which officials were to be gathered about Norris for the arrival photos. They then retired to a separate booth to talk shop.

On the train, George Norris could hear the porter awakening late sleepers as he fixed his bow tie. Standing before a mirror on a moving train, he thought, is quite a task. Shaving, he had already decided, was nothing short of taking your life in your own hands.

Norris didn't have to worry about fitting last-minute speech manuscript revisions into his always-overflowing briefcase. He had no prepared speech. His views had been heard and judged, he thought. But the trusty old briefcase remained near.

Norris thought of several possible ways of greeting the reported mob at the depot. He realized that many of those on hand would be among his closest friends and most loyal supporters who had come to sympathize. Likewise, he knew that some might be opponents who had come to scorn.

Should he tell them that it's good to be going home to southwest Nebraska, or should he speak the blunt, painful truth? He pondered; Ellie watched.

The time was at hand.

St. Louis was an emotional pilgrimage for George Norris. Here he could see one of his fondest dreams blossom—for he truly was its father.

Norris now paused to consider the thoughts of George Aiken as he reviewed a text of the senator's speech scheduled for delivery the next night.

Aiken had written:

The REA has laid the foundation for a better rural life. . . . Rural electric lines wind their way into communities previously unserved, bringing better living and more efficient production to these localities. The rural power line is a necessity.

Today in Washington I see them working to prevent any further extension of rural advantages, except those which they control.

The thunder of clapping hands would roll as Senator Aiken concluded:

9

We have seen titles to the great natural resources of our nation so manipulated by corporate organizations and cartels that today the transportation, the power, the products of our mines, the commerce of our seas, and the financial policies of our nation are ultimately controlled by less than one percent of the people.

We see this right before us. Even those who are themselves in control see it. Many of them recognize such a condition as leading only to ultimate disaster and would themselves correct it if they could. We are challenged with the problem of working out a better system and putting it into operation. To meet this challenge will require all of our resourcefulness and courage.

Suddenly, Norris could hear the drawling voice of John Rankin.

There is enough water power now going to waste in our navigable streams and their tributaries to electrify every home in America, including every farm home, and supply them with ample current for cooking, heating and refrigeration," Rankin was contending.

The object of our power program is to get that power developed and then, through the REA, get it distributed to every farm home in America, at rates the farmer can afford to pay.

The power business is a public business. Electricity now has become a necessity of life.

This time it was George Norris doing the applauding.

And now, the President's representative was at the rostrum delivering a personal message from FDR:

I wish that you would also express by appreciation of the importance of such an association, representing hundreds of thousands of farmers who have joined on a cooperative basis to assure their families the economic and social advantages of plentiful electricity at low rates.

Year by year, through REA reports, I have followed the advance of rural pole lines, like a peaceful army, to the conquest of a better life for those who produce the nation's basic agricultural products.

Today, the scores of electric devices, performing essential farm operations, are also potent implements for winning the war. Production and preservation of food have become of critical importance to the defense of democracy.

Thus, the extension of electric service to a million farms was an important step in preparedness for ultimate victory. As the strain of manpower grows, the nation will realize ever more clearly how much the rural electrification cooperatives have added to its strength.

Norris nodded.

Words like these from his friend in the White House comforted Norris. For even though he would be unable to carry on the fight, Roosevelt would still be there. And, for as long as Franklin Roosevelt was President, Norris knew REA would be in safe hands.

As the cheering subsided and delegates were taking their seats, Norris started to tell the story of REA. "Honest work done in behalf of our fellow men, as we struggle along in this imperfect world, is the best and only pay for a lifetime of work," he began. "It goes further and deeper into the human soul and the human heart than any kind of compensation could go. I hope I may, during the few remaining days of my life, do nothing that will cause regret from you for what you have done for me tonight." Forcefully, he continued: "There never should be a drop of water come from the heavens and fall upon the earth beneath unless it does some good to man."

Recalling the quarrel over initial REA legislation, Norris took his listeners back to the conference committee designated to iron out differences between the two houses of Congress. Intense disagreement erupted over two issues. They were whether patronage would be employed in REA and whether interest on REA loans should be allowed to exceed 3 percent. When the deadlock persisted, Norris stomped out with a warning. "Don't forget that this question of Rural Electrification Administration is going to the voters of the United States," Norris had shouted. "It is going to be an issue in the next campaign. I think I can make it an issue, and I am going to have a lot of help to do that."

The senator was particularly unbending on the interest proposition.

When the smoke had cleared, Norris emerged the victor. "My own opinion, my own private opinion, is that the government on this great undertaking could afford to loan the money for nothing," he argued. "It ought to loan it without any interest. We have subsidized everybody in creation where it didn't do anybody but a few people any good."

Wrinkles in his brow deepened as he warned: "I want to call your attention to the fact that the man who is opposed to the electric development, improvement of our natural resources, I think, has something wrong about him somewhere, even though he goes to church every Sunday and pays the preacher well, and leads in prayer meeting every Thursday night."

Linking REA to the original public power developments in the Tennessee Valley, Norris hammered home his final point:

You cannot separate these things. They belong together. God put them together.

And, every stream that rolls down the mountainside through the meadows into the sea ought to be made to bring its blessings, its comforts, its joys, to the farm home as well as to the city home.

On Nebraska farms that night, lamps lighted the senator's trail home.

Three

The train rolled west across the snow-clad fields of Missouri.

Winter can be deadly in the Plains—and this January morning was ominously cold and windy. More fresh snow could quickly turn it into the winter nightmare that midwestern stockmen dread.

Back in St. Louis, activity at the Jefferson Hotel was again in full swing. Rural electric delegates were in the midst of the final day of their first national conclave. There were many who spoke of the spectacle of the night before.

On the train, Ellie gazed down at the shining silver salute—George William's REA plaque. She had carried it aboard, and she would be its custodian for the final day's journey. She would place it on the mantle in the front room at McCook, a constant reminder that his work had not gone unseen. Ellie knew the plaque would mean much to George William in the days ahead.

At the window, an old man watched Missouri roll by. But he was in Tennessee, sweeping down the valley by train for a triumphant tour of the infant TVA. It wasn't January; it was June. It wasn't cold, but rather hot. And he was no longer old.

Ellie was at his side—and Jack and Hazel, too. He wanted very much to see how work was progressing on the dams, whether the vast project was really on schedule and just how the massive program was being implemented. He loved the valley, and he enjoyed the warmth of its people. He had always drawn inspiration and satisfaction from previous visits. But he didn't know that this was to be his last.

The senator smiled as the train snorted to a stop by a little white sign simply marked "Norris." For now they had arrived at the little construction town named for its founder. Here, the Nebraskan would always be at home.

The luggage was barely off the train when a local newspaper photographer called for a family line-up to check the accuracy of his camera. There stood Jack, Hazel, Ellie, and George William, all reluctantly smiling into the hot sun.

Then, without warning, a portly woman—probably in her mid-forties—barged to the front of the focal shutter demanding that her picture be taken with the senator. Caught off guard, Norris uttered a hesitant okay while stoking up a fresh cigar for the occasion. Meanwhile, the family took the cue and escaped under the drooping arms of a nearby shade tree to observe. The somewhat rattled photographer had a pair of wide grins to capture.

Open expressions of sentiment—as this one—were not uncommon for the man Tennessee Valley residents referred to as "Uncle George." Walls of eating houses, general stores, and personal dwellings displayed pictures of Norris. Tennesseans, whether rich or poor, white or black, felt strongly about their visitor.

Now, blocking his path to the inviting shade tree was a big, burly construction worker who bellowed: "My, but you look a lot like George Norris, stranger."

Calmly, Norris peered around, hoping that no one else had heard the man, and whispered in a confidential tone: "You know, more people tell me that." Chuckling to himself, George William pushed on for the tree, leaving the unsuspecting worker scratching his chin.

Again, the family observed with grins.

This was typical George Norris. At no time during his forty-year tenure in politics did he go out of his way for personal recognition; rather, he shied away from it. Yet he never let a personal greeting—whether from friend or foe—fall on deaf ears.

The valley was particularly lovely this trip. Never had Norris seen it so green. Where yawning gulleys once were, now green sod reclined. Precious topsoil would no longer ride the rainwaters down the valley. The marks of erosion and waste were already disappearing. Truly, the blessings of controlled resource development were popping up everywhere.

At Doctor Morgan's cabin, the heat was less oppressive. The Norris clan moved in with little effort—and Hazel cast a gleaming eye at the nearby lake. But the senator had no time to waste. He was already back in the car, ready for the long-awaited look at progress on Norris Dam.

The sight was awesome. Men moved about the great structure like an army of ants, building a future for the Tennessee Valley. The noise was terrific, and streams of sweat flowed down from the silver helmets, which reflected the summer sun.

As Norris moved by, workmen occasionally turned about to nod or smile. Where conversation would not unduly delay the proceedings, Norris would stop and chat a bit. Many of the men had seen him before on earlier visits. Some asked who the distinguished onlooker was. But not a one failed to recognize the name—for it was his dam that they were building.

Norris moved from project to project—checking the area where cement blocks were created, the powerhouse, the storage grounds, the central checking area. He looked; he walked; he inquired. Seemingly nothing escaped his eye—for this was his dream coming true. He was awake, and, he thought to himself, so at last was the valley.

This would be an example to the entire world, Norris knew.

Here, one could see what benefit might be harvested from public ownership and control over the forces of nature. Flood control, navigation, and power development would all be pursued in order. And the result, Norris believed, would be prosperity for the valley. More than that, he hoped—an example to the nation, the first of many such multipurpose projects.

Shades of twilight brought Hazel from the lake's cooling waters, Ellie and Mrs. Morgan from the bustling village, and Jack, Morgan, and George William from the scene of growth.

The spacious Morgan cabin rang loudly with laughter and words of excitement. But the topic never swayed from TVA. At the dinner table, Norris sandwiched bits of TVA in with generous slabs of roast beef. Meticulously outlining tomorrow's day of sightseeing was Norris's trusted colleague and host, Doctor H. A. Morgan, a member of the TVA board. Eyes widened with anticipation as the doctor told of the tour, which would begin at the break of dawn. They would see the dam and tour the valley downstream. They would survey the tentative sites of new TVA projects—and they would climb the mountain. At last, Norris would have an opportunity to talk to many of the people who had spoken to him through crudely penciled notes.

The day would be a high adventure for George Norris, for it would provide an opportunity to observe the present while peering into the future. Norris had seen the past—and it had not been pleasing to him. On this day, he could take the people's pulse, explore with them the change that was transforming this valley into a land of hope.

While the tour was carefully planned, time gaps were left open for Norris to fill as he wished. Morgan would be the guide, but the senator would remain the boss. They would go where Norris wished to go, linger where he wanted to stop, and depart from the trip's itinerary if and when the senator wished to stray.

The valley's potential had hardly been tapped, Norris and Morgan agreed. They were already discussing what might be next, for it was always the future that concerned George Norris. The past was dead. Once the work of the present was properly undertaken, it was to the future that the senator turned. In that distant land, there were always new obstacles to overcome, problems to conquer.

As Morgan completed the outline of the next day's tour, Norris stepped outside to view a carpet of stars in the dark sky. Inside, the doctor replaced his papers in the briefcase. The trip was set.

Something tugged at George Norris as he breathed deeply of the soft breeze. He must, he decided, have another look at the great dam site before bed.

Ellie, Jack, Hazel all piled into Morgan's car with the senator. As they rode through the night toward Norris Dam, an air of expectancy gripped them. And as the car drew nearer, the hammering noise of work on the vast project echoed through the still cool air. It grew louder.

Then, suddenly, as they rounded the last curve, the night became day again. The entire area was bathed in floodlight. Ants still moved about the huge structure; only now they were followed by tiny shadows. The dam itself never looked larger, an imposing lighted wall standing erect and powerful against the inky Tennessee night. Norris blinked at the bright sight. His eyes narrowed as he stared into the illuminated scene.

What had seemed overpowering in the daytime was now plainly overwhelming. It was Ellie who gasped. Jack's jaw dropped; Hazel smiled. And it was George William's cheek that grew moist in the evening air.

Four

As the shrill construction whistle signaled the hour, morning-shift workers took their posts. Shuffling off the job, lunch pails in hand, moved the weary night crew. Standing to one side, watching the morning ritual, was the dark-suited, bow-tied visitor.

His glasses reflected the early morning sun. Awkwardly perched atop his white hair was a shining protective helmet, tilting slightly over one ear. Under an arm, he balanced charts and papers that he would use on the day's tour. In one hand, a cigar smoldered in the heavy morning air. Gathered about the intent figure were his host, his administrative assistant, and their three ladies deep in conversation.

Thus began George Norris's long-awaited day in the valley.

Soon the car was moving into the country, where the sound of birds on the wing replaced the deep voices of machines at work. Towering steel-framed giants holding the power of the valley dwarfed the passersby. As far as the eye could see, electric transmission lines were silhouetted against the sky. The offspring of the TVA, they were ready to transport the power harnessed by the dams to homes all across the valley—and especially to farm homes, Norris thought.

Across the road, barges moved silently along the river. Soon, the senator told Doctor Morgan, larger craft would tread that channel. Land near the river's bank was barren. But, Norris knew, it could soon become green again—no longer the innocent victim of flooding waters. Trees hugged the shoreline, quenching their thirst along the placid stream. A program of reforestation would strengthen their numbers, Morgan informed.

Here and there, the senator's good friend would point out the tentative sites of new industry. Many plants were anxious to share in the valley's new prosperity. Much industrial expansion was in the wind.

A farmer waved as the auto moved on. Fields were lush. And farm wives were anxiously awaiting the advent of the connecting line that would rush a new servant into their homes.

Sailboats floated across a distant lake.

What a marvelous sight, Norris reflected. The people of the valley were caught in the magic grip of growing prosperity. And the pleasant prospect was more of the same. What growth, what healthful growth, Norris marveled as the valley passed by in colorful review. He smiled and thought how beautiful this once destitute baby of the New Deal had grown to be since its birth in 1933. The baby had outgrown the crib and was now walking as an adult.

How the senator wished that early opponents of the baby's adoption could be here today. He wished that they could view the tremendous growth and accomplishments in navigation, flood control, power development and distribution, new and better fertilizers, agricultural advances, erosion control, and reforestation. Norris felt much as a father at his son's high school graduation. He reflects joy, but at the same time recalls the difficult years of childhood.

He thought of the days when he headed the Senate Committee on Agriculture and Forestry. After World War I, a great debate was ignited over the use of government-built plants in the Tennessee Valley. More specifically, Norris recalled the long and heated tussle over the fate of Wilson Dam at Muscle Shoals. Chemical companies, power outlets, and other private business enterprises made offers to take the dam and nearby munitions plants off the government's hands at "bargain prices."

Instead, Norris proposed that the Muscle Shoals properties be operated publicly. With the national economy on the upturn, Congress passed the Norris bill only to have it pocket-vetoed by President Coolidge in 1928. In 1930 another Norris bill was passed. This time it was President Hoover who applied the veto.

But in 1932 the unborn TVA baby found a foster father. Franklin D. Roosevelt was elected President. And in 1933, backed by Roosevelt, the third Norris bill was passed and signed into being.

Doctor Morgan could remember the day. With fruit crates serving as chairs in a barren Washington hotel room, the TVA board met for the first time on June 16, 1933. The doctor was a member of that board.

Since that time, the baby had developed through eight turbulent peacetime years. With pride, Norris looked on as the grown child donned khaki.

The TVA constructed a new synthetic ammonia plant during World War II and reconditioned its World War I ammonium nitrate facilities at Muscle Shoals to produce explosives. It aided immeasurably in providing electric power for a nation engulfed in the strain and pain of world conflict.

Thus, Norris thought to himself, the TVA had served the valley in peacetime, and was now enlisted as a weapon of war. It would once again return to its valued peacetime role when the battle was won. It was proving itself with every passing day.

Back at the cabin, the men left their ladies. Then, they pushed up the road toward the mountain. The June sun was a hazy glare as they moved round and round up the mountainside. The hot summer air grew almost cool. The river below became an ever thinner ribbon.

Easing to a halt near the top, Morgan hopped out of the vehicle and waited for Norris. The senator straightened his tie and they walked toward the edge.

Suddenly, a new world unfolded before their eyes. Below, the Tennessee River had become a winding, shimmering string. A jigsaw puzzle of green and brown outlined the fields. Like drops of water, lakes dotted the countryside. Forested areas blotted out much of the land below. Here and there, cement lines carried moving dots across the land. The site of construction at Norris Dam was but a tiny spot.

It struck Norris all at once. How small the huge dam appeared from way up here. It was, he saw, but a little part of the entire picture. And that, the senator thought to himself, was exactly what it was. Often, you must get far away from something to really see it in perspective. Norris Dam was only one small project in the entire TVA development, and the TVA itself might be just the small beginning of similar expansion across the breadth of the nation and the expanse of the globe.

Toward the bottom of the long, winding mountain road, the car came to a chugging stop. At the side of a rocky path, a string of black children waved to "Uncle George."

Norris's head popped out of the window for a closer look. The shoeless greeters shied away. Norris recognized them with a smile.

Again, their nerve and enthusiasm returned as they frantically waved, "So long, Uncle George."

The car now had gathered its second wind, and in a huff, it rambled on. The view from the mountain was permanently imprinted on the senator's mind. He had seen much of the 41,000-square mile valley region in one glance. The valley spread into seven states. In its confines dwelled 3½ million people. Each had already felt the impact of TVA. Power would in time flow from thirty-one multipurpose dams into eighty thousand square miles of the South.

Norris knew only too well that a mere 3.5 percent of the valley's farm were electrified when the TVA took form. The percentage had zoomed skyward ever since, and the senator looked hopefully ahead to the day when nine out of ten valley farm homes would be lighted.

And that wasn't all. Fifteen thousand people found direct employment with the TVA; thousands of others were employed in industries that emerged as a result of the valley's development.

The eventful day had thrilled George Norris. He had seen first-hand the benefits he had envisioned for so long. Now he was anxious to return to the cabin where he could relax and review the day's marvels with the family. Norris was hurrying home in Morgan's car when it happened.

"Next stop, Kansas City!"

Bursting out of nowhere, tearing the treasured past from his mind came the train conductor's shout that blotted out all the joy of traveling the Tennessee Valley. For Kansas City was not in the valley.

Five

It was cold out on the barren brick platform. Norris and Ellie peered up and down the long deserted trackside, hunting in vain for a redcap. They shivered in the chilly winter air. At their feet rested three bulging grips. Ellie held firmly onto the plaque.

They had hoped to keep the same compartment for the final night's journey through Nebraska, so it had been with considerable disappointment that they vacated their quarters at the request of the conductor. But it was wartime, and the inconvenience of unscheduled train changes, missing redcaps, and tardy arrivals could be borne without complaint.

Standing deserted in the brisk moist Kansas City air, Ellie worried, was not the best thing for George William.

Suddenly, a trainman beckoned them to follow his pointing finger. It seemed that their car had been switched over to the train going to Omaha and McCook. It was, he told them, way down there—at the end of the long string of coaches and Pullmans.

Burdened with two suitcases and his briefcase, Norris trudged along beside Ellie, who, at George William's insistence, carried the lightest bag. It must have been the longest train in Missouri, the senator assured himself as they arrived panting and weary at the steps of their car. Once inside the compartment, the tired twosome slouched in their seats. They would rest before unpacking the luggage loaded not so many minutes ago. Norris couldn't help but ponder the old expression. Yes, he thought, what a way to run a railroad.

Now, they were ready to move north. They would roll through Nebraska during the night, arriving at home early the next morning, probably before dawn. Ellie wondered what the homecoming would be like.

McCook was their home, the only place in the world that George William ever considered his home. Of course, they had been in Washington much more of the time, and often most of the summer had been consumed at the cottage on the lakes in Wisconsin. But McCook was home.

Norris dearly loved the people there. After all, it was they who had elected him as their district judge so many years ago. It was they and their neighbors who had honored him with five terms in the House. And the entire state had five times granted him the privilege of serving in the nation's highest legislative office—that of a U.S. senator. They were his people, and for forty years he had been their servant.

The air was fresh in McCook. If the summer days were hot, they were at least dry, and evenings were cool and refreshing.

There was room to move in McCook. Washington was always a mob, a crush of important people in a hurry, a crowd of ambitious men only too often bumping and pushing and clawing their way to the top. People were callously tricked, tripped, and walked upon in Washington every day. In McCook the pace was calm; the people were kind.

Home is where the heart is. And whether in the nation's capital, in the Tennessee Valley, in Wisconsin, or anywhere in the land, George Norris left his heart in McCook.

And so it was a darting pain that ripped his heart as he unfolded the creased and wrinkled newspaper clipping. Norris had looked at it many times before. It was dated November 4, 1942. It bore the familiar type of the *McCook Daily Gazette*. It mercilessly shouted its message at him once again. In cold, cruel print, it lashed his eyes.

Kenneth S. Wherry (R), 782.
Foster May (D), 152.
George W. Norris (I), 659.

He winced as the McCook city election figures punctured his heart.

To lose Nebraska was bad enough. To have lost the support of his own neighbors, the people he counted as his own, was unbearable. He had decided he would never ask why. For no reason could be reason enough. No excuse or explanation from friends could suffice. Nothing could erase the fact—or ease the grief.

Norris had decided during the last eleven weeks that the verdict was clear: he and all his work had been rejected. An entire lifetime of public service had been judged. For some reason, he had been found lacking. He had placed his record on the line for approval—it had been disapproved. Norris folded the clipping, tucked it away and prepared for bed.

Ellie had seen the brow furrow, the eyes tighten, the shoulders sink. She knew what was in that scrap of paper. And she knew what it was doing to George William. What Ellie could not foresee—and she had tried often during the long trek from Washington—was what lay ahead in McCook. What would the morrow bring?

She had written their old and trusted friend Carl Marsh. She had told him when they would arrive, knowing that he would warm the furnace and open the house. It was a great comfort to know that Carl would be there, but he was all that she could depend on. The remainder of the next day's events was shrouded in mystery.

Norris was asleep when the train rolled across the border into Nebraska. At Omaha, sleepy-eyed travelers boarded the late-arriving coaches carrying newspapers under their arms. An Omaha paper fell into the aisle as one weary passenger slumped into deep sleep. Later, a porter glanced at it under the dim bulb near the restroom and read of the impassioned address of Nebraska's defeated senator in St. Louis.

He recalled the old man's years of service, and wondered where the returning warrior might be this very night.

A few cars down the track, Norris rolled over on his side. Ellie opened one eye and listened. He was resting well, she assured herself.

In McCook that night, Norris's friends had gone to bed early.

Six

"I was defeated. It was the democratic way that I have always advocated for forty years. My people made their choice."

George Norris looked intently back at the sea of faces that met his eyes, and continued.

Turning to the war and the future of the world when it was at peace again, he thundered: "If we are to repeat the mistakes we made before—mistakes like the one at Versailles—then, we had better die. . . . If we are going to repeat this every generation, then we'd better give up civilization."

He is doing remarkably well, Ellie thought as she looked up at him. Ellie had feared what his reaction to this homecoming banquet might be. Would it shred his heart, or soothe it? Would he accept the hometown tribute with gratitude, or would it only serve to imprint defeat more deeply on his broken life?

She looked out over the audience. Here, in the main floor dining room of the Keystone Hotel, flanked by pillars and arranged in a semicircle sat the senator's McCook friends. A number of invited out-of-town guests, particularly public power representatives, filled the remaining seats. Attendance had been limited to 150 persons, partially because of wartime rationing. That number would also fill the dining hall.

"We must seek a peace that will be welcomed by the millions yet unborn and innocent of anything that brought this terrible war about," he continued. "I regret that I have been deprived of that right [to help write the peace], but I can't complain. That right was taken away by my own people in the truly democratic way. I am relieved of a great responsibility."

The banquet, Ellie recalled, had begun at 6:30 p.m. That meant it had now been going for two hours. Good, she thought. George William would be finished in a bit. Frank Colfer, the toastmaster, would then move into the group singing—and George William would be home in time to get his usual eight hours of sleep. Ellie relaxed more.

"The fight against the TVA goes on. I'm out of it now. I'm out to stay . . . my people took me out. They had that right. They're the kings. I'm not complaining, even if I am sorrowful, but I hope this fight goes on to a successful conclusion, and I know it will. I want to see the TVA multiplied a thousand times all over the world, not in this country alone. I hope I can look down from the beyond and see it done someday."

Norris's voice carried well in the high-ceilinged, echo-infested banquet room. For once, the usually distracting acoustics did not seem to irritate the attentive listeners.

Lying before the dollar-a-plate diners was the hotel's best linen, some of which was imported from Europe. The linen seemed extra fresh and bright for the evening's festivities. The clear glass chandeliers cast shadows on the varied array of facial features. Dark, double-breasted suits were the attire for the evening. Smoke hung heavy in the hall, but the opening of windows drew cold disapproval from the diners. In the background, the smell of coffee seeped through the kitchen doors.

At the head table, Gerald Gentleman applauded. Ellie leaned forward and smiled down at him. Mr. Gentleman had delivered the nicest, the most eloquent, and the grandest tribute of all this night, Ellie thought to herself.

What was it he had said? Well, she remembered, he had said something about the rich mixture of honesty, rugged individualism, a deep sense of dedication and true humility. A great man, yet a humble man. That's what he had said.

And he recalled the continual displays of honor and statesmanship in the stately old battler. At the same time, he marveled at the senator's deep-seated abilities of logic and evaluation. "A remarkable man," Gentleman nodded.

Gentleman was just then thinking to himself how true his words had been. He had been invited to attend the affair as general manager of the Platte Valley Public Power and Irrigation District at North Platte. But he had not expected to speak. So when he was called upon suddenly, the words that flowed forth formed in the heart and somehow made their way to his mouth. They had come easily, he thought, for they expressed accurately his sentiments about George Norris.

Gentleman had known the senator for some time. He had been Platte Valley's general manager for more than five years. He could well remember when the district was having difficulty snagging a federal appropriation of something over $1 million. He just wasn't getting anywhere with the request, so he went to McCook and sought out the senator. He explained the need. He sadly reported that he was having no luck in Washington. Norris, he recalled, just listened. He did not indicate he would help. But the senator returned to Congress in January, and Platte Valley had its money in February.

Gentlemen remembered visiting the senator in Washington. There was no superficial display of importance at the Senate Office Building, no cooling of the heels, no false show of power. Norris was easy to talk to. He made no promises. He listened and he questioned—but he gave no guarantees, pledged no support. Yet you knew that if you had convinced him you were right, he would come to your aid. And before long, you would have what you had asked.

Gentleman recalled once offering, with a grin, a ten-cent cigar to the senator. He had taken it, and he had said: "That's what I smoke." Gentleman smiled as he remembered that. Noticing the grin, down the table, Ellie smiled back.

The TVA, Norris was saying, is basically a matter of "putting the water and soil together."

It struck a responsive chord with Gentleman. He remembered how Norris would come the seventy-five miles from McCook to North Platte to inspect the district properties. Once, he had seen where water had been allowed to eat gulleys around some of the facilities. "Those things ought to be fixed properly before they get worse," Gentleman remembered the senator saying. Norris was very observant. He would get out of the car and carefully view whatever was up for consideration. When he saw something that displeased him, he asked or he suggested. Norris had always admonished him—and other Nebraska public power men—to "keep the cost down, keep the price right." That's what they would always try to do.

It seemed to Gentleman that the senator was most proud of the REA and its blessings. Norris had always seemed to be most interested in "getting power out to the farmers." That task had appeared to be his driving force, his mission, his life's goal. Had Norris been successful? Gentleman rubbed his chin. Let's see, back when the Rural Electrification Act became law, about 4 percent of Nebraska's farm homes were electrified. Tonight, while George Norris was speaking, perhaps 40 percent of the farm homes in the vast Cornhusker State were lit. Gentleman could easily look ahead to the day when the figure would be 95 percent—for the connecting lines were spreading daily. A great cobweb was engulfing the state, carrying power in its threads. New farms were being lit every night.

Meanwhile, the clerk in the hotel's adjoining cigar store was left deserted among the stacks of magazines and newspapers. Talk of the Yankees, Bob Feller's blazing fastball, Marty Marion's deadly peg from shortstop to first base, and the Cardinals' chances for the approaching season was stranded at second. The group of hot stove leaguers had tiptoed across the deserted lobby and were pressing near the closed banquet room door. They heard frequent clapping of hands and an occasional chuckle from the senator.

The cigar store "regulars" took turns reviewing their experiences with the speaker. One told how he had "advised" the senator on the growing evils of big business. Another told how Norris sought his views on possible ways of strengthening the REA in Red Willow County and Nebraska. And still another told how "Norris listened to every word I ever told him and he never talked back." Soon, however, the talk again revolved about who would be batting cleanup for the Yankees come opening day.

Inside, Carl Marsh looked up at Norris. Introducing his friend had been a great honor, Marsh thought to himself. What a needless sacrifice for the nation not to have his wisdom enter into the writing of the peace, Marsh was thinking. On the way to the Keystone, Marsh had checked the evening paper. It was filled with the news that Roosevelt and Churchill had just completed a historic conference at Casablanca. Already, the terms of peace were being considered. Unconditional surrender was in the air.

"I want to stand before you long enough to say that in all those years of service, my lips have never told a lie and my hands have never touched a bribe."

To the ringing applause of his listeners, now on their feet, George Norris took his seat.

Seven

As he leaned forward to strike a match against the red brick fireplace in the front room at 706 Main, thoughts of summer—and Wisconsin—came flowing back to George Norris. It was the brick that touched off this newest sojourn into the past.

"The dealer made a mistake," Norris could remember himself telling Ellie.

They were standing over a large stack of red bricks that had just been unloaded in front of their summer cottage at Point Comfort. "Now, we'll have these bricks taken back if you wish," Norris was saying.

Ellie had wanted the fireplace at their cottage to be constructed of natural stone. George William had wanted brick. At last, Norris had told Ellie they would go ahead with her plans for the stone.

But now as she looked down at the imposing pile of neatly stacked bricks, Ellie smilingly thought: A sweetly executed maneuver. No, she told George William, the bricks would do fine. And to his continuing protests that the lumber dealer had erred in filling their order, she thought silently: Indeed.

Norris broke into a wide grin, lit his pipe, and eased into his rocker. As the first puffs of smoke circled skyward, the senator's mind was again at Haleiwa. That was the name of the large cottage Norris had constructed in east-central Wisconsin lake country, five miles west of the little resort town of Waupaca. The name was Hawaiian. It meant "beautiful place." Norris had come in contact with the word on a congressional delegation visit to Hawaii, and the cottage had really been named before it was built.

Norris had owned the land on Point Comfort since 1905, and a cottage had been the dream of both Ellie and George William from that date on. In 1921, the dream became reality, and they began their annual summer retreats at Haleiwa.

Here, Norris found the perfect hideaway, a place where he could rest and think, far away from the rigors of official Washington. Here, the wonders of rural electrification and the potentialities of controlled river development were to crystalize in his imagination.

Wisconsin would be his place of relaxation, but the senator's active mind continued its work even when he was lying on the lawn flat on his back smoking a cigar under the evergreens.

Norris had labored alongside the carpenters and masons when they constructed the summer cottage. Each summer, he would add carpentry work of his own, improving the cottage's interior to his own specifications.

Mornings in Wisconsin began with a swim in the channel outside the front door. Norris was in the water on cool mornings and warm. A breakfast of hotcakes and maple syrup followed.

Then, the senator would often work outside, watering the lawn, trimming trees, or doing other necessary chores. The cottage was surrounded on three sides by water. Rainbow Lake lay just outside the side door. Woods overlooked the back of the structure.

Half submerged in water and mud, Norris would frantically push and pull mounting debris from under the boathouse. The more mud speckled his arms and face, the harder he would toil, until finally the boathouse again stood on clear waters. Then, after an hour or so, the tired statesman would emerge on dry land with water streaming from his boots like salt from a shaker. The big black rubber boots, he often chuckled, didn't quite measure up to the "eloquently worded guarantee." The boathouse episode was an almost daily ritual.

By now, the hungry senator's thoughts were on a freshly cut side of Wisconsin mountain cheese. So, with his hat in hand, George William and Ellie were gone.

Across the scenic countryside, the Norris car could be spotted from time to time as it sped toward the neighboring cheese factory. The strong scent served effectively as a road marker. Once there, Norris wasted little time in striking a bargain after nibbling a rich, yellow sample. Several fresh cheese cakes rode back with the Nebraska shoppers. Often, George William and Ellie would split the twenty-five-mile trip by halting under a shade tree with healthy portions of cheese in hand.

As long as they were out and there were several hours of sunlight left, Ellie suggested another stop, this time for maple syrup. She explained that the supply at the cabin had been dwindling heavily in recent mornings. Norris agreed, visualizing a stack of Ellie's hot cakes bathed in heavy portions of syrup and butter.

Often, Norris would drive into Waupaca for groceries, or he visited with neighboring farmers along the lake. Ellie and he might go for a drive in the countryside.

Or they would go boating. The senator didn't like the canoe very well, but he did enjoy the rowboat. Sometimes both he and Ellie would row; other times, Norris alone manned the oars.

Now and then, they would hunt arrowheads on the nearby grounds. In this Indian country, Norris had once discovered an old battle-ax, which they now used as a paperweight.

The senator enjoyed the isolation of the cottage. Located between two paved roads, it could be reached by winding down the little old country path known as Smith's Lane. It could also be found by boat; in later years, the stacks of summer Norris mail came by marine delivery.

Ellie and the senator often read to each other in the evening. They consumed *Gone with the Wind* in that manner one summer. They started to read *Grapes of Wrath* another time, but he didn't finish it.

Norris might doze in a hammock in the cool evening air, or sit on the porch, a cigar in his mouth and his feet on the railing. The *Chicago Tribune* and stacks of Nebraska newspapers often surrounded him. A stenographer would handle the senator's mail. Later, Jack Robertson would come to lend a hand.

Outside, evergreens, pine, white birch, and weeping willows stood guard. Norris planted the birch himself.

The cottage had no telephone—that's the way Norris wanted it. To reach the senator by phone in the summer, one would call the resort hotel across the channel or the Wisconsin Soldiers Home across Rainbow Lake. Word of the call was often relayed to the cottage by voice. "Norris, Norris!" echoed through the woods. Other times, a messenger would deliver the news. Norris would hop in his rowboat and proceed across the waters to answer. A quick row across the lake took fifteen or twenty minutes; the hotel could be reached in five or six minutes.

Often, Norris would go to the Soldiers Home at King just to visit. He had many friends in the little community, including Edwin Smith, the postmaster. The senator knew all the shopkeepers, and occasionally they would visit for an hour or more.

Before the post office provided mail delivery by boat, Norris traveled to King to pick up his usual bundle of letters. He had mail every day, sometimes as many as three dozen pieces. He dictated return correspondence to Jack or a stenographer from the rocking chair on the porch.

The cottage was large and comfortable, arranged in just the order the senator desired. Four bedrooms and one bathroom filled the upstairs; a living room, dining room, kitchen, and bath spread through the first floor. The porch was open on three sides and afforded a breathtaking view of the lakeland.

Evenings were cool, and often the oil heater in the kitchen and the fireplace were set aflame. Blankets were in order at bedtime. Despite the chill, Norris often took an evening swim before the sun faded out of sight for another night.

The senator's birthdays were often observed at the cottage in July.

Norris could remember well the year of the green Wedgewood bowl. Ellie had seen a beautiful bowl that she wanted very much for herself. It seemed that George William's birthday was coming up. Ellie bought the bowl; George William received it for his birthday. Norris had laughed and laughed. And he impatiently awaited Ellie's next birthday. When it came, she unwrapped a daintily ribboned saw.

Sometimes, Norris would go fishing in Wisconsin. He didn't like to fish, but he would go just to be neighborly. He liked to build birdhouses, or grab the walking cane for a trip into the woods.

Wisconsin was a second wind for George Norris, a place to renew his strength for battles that lay ahead. It was in Wisconsin that he envisioned the course he would take. His resolve was bolstered by the woods and the water. Uncertainty faded under the evergreens; hesitation vanished in the cool lake.

What wonderful times they had at the cottage, Norris recalled. On this chilly winter night in McCook, he wished that summer would come again. He ached for the comfort and the peace that were his in Wisconsin. But he knew that he would never again be entirely at peace. He suspected that he would never see the cottage again. Wisconsin, Haleiwa, Port Comfort were all gone forever.

Norris tapped the smoldering remnants from his empty pipe. They fell into a small heap and collapsed in the ashtray.

Eight

As the President completed his fireside report to the nation, George Norris flicked off his radio. Not so long ago, he would have been just a matter of blocks from the White House when the message was delivered. Now, he was a thousand miles away. He was not so many months earlier able to help transform the President's words into action on the floor of the Senate. He could lend a hand. Now, he was no longer a senator, no longer in a position to aid. He might have been informed of the President's thoughts before the speech and shared in the exchange of ideas that preceded its delivery. Now, he could no longer counsel.

Roosevelt's words took Norris back to December 10, 1942. It was 7:30 p.m. and the senator was seated at the head table in the ballroom at the Mayflower Hotel in Washington. The affair was a stag dinner, and Norris was its honored guest.

Senator Joseph F. Guffey, dinner host, was reading a telegram, addressed to George W. Norris, which read:

Dear George: You can understand, I am sure, why it isn't possible for me to attend dinners these days. Nor do I need to tell you of the pleasure it would give me to be with the friends who are gathering in your honor tonight.

It would ever be a privilege as well as a pleasure to join with any group of fellow Americans whose purpose is to recognize your long and faithful service as guardian of the public interest. Of all that you have done for your country and for your fellow citizens as the tireless champion of liberalism, I have spoken many times publicly and privately.

Through two score years you have been as a tower of strength in every storm. I can only reiterate what I have often said before that in our national history we have had few elder statesmen who, like you, have preserved the aspirations of youth as they accumulated the wisdom of years.

In these critical days we need your counsel as never before and the youth of the land particularly need the force of your example which has been as a beacon light of righteousness for more than a generation.

Always affectionately, Franklin D. Roosevelt.

The senator's friends, all in business suits, applauded.

It was a mild December night. Norris had been driven from his residence at the Dodge Hotel to the Mayflower by Jack Robertson. It had been five weeks since his defeat, and Norris was becoming accustomed to it. So were the illustrious guests at the hotel—but they didn't like it. This evening was to ring with pleas to Norris not to turn from public service.

It was a serious moment. The liberals were fearful, the progressives disturbed. With George Norris might go a raft of social programs, both active and future. The election of 1942 was a bitter pill for Democrats, and the loss of one of their dearest heroes only served to magnify their distress.

Twenty-two senators were in attendance; the vice president was there; five justices of the Supreme Court were on hand, as well as the Speaker of the House.

Senator Guffey continued to read wires and messages from across the nation. The notes came from all places and people.

Here is one from Cordell Hull:

> No one has more greatly admired than I the courage, integrity, broad vision, and constructive statesmanship displayed by Senator Norris throughout his entire career.

Here is one from the Secretary of the Interior:

> His days of leadership of the just cause will cease only with his death, and down the pages of history long, long after that he will continue to be an inspiration to those who believe that the rights of man are worth fighting for.
> —Harold L. Ickes.

Here is one from the South:

> The name of George Norris is imperishably a part of our improved Constitution, the reformation of parliamentary practices, the preservation of water power for the benefit of all the people and all forward-looking achievements of his generation.
>
> Full of years and full of honors, he retires from Congress but not from service for the weal of his countrymen. His courage, vision, and independence constitute a trinity of virtues, which, added to his exemplification of the simple life, make him the commanding figure in an era of change and progress.
> —Josephus Daniels, Raleigh, N.C.

Here is one from Kansas:

> I know of no other man in the United States who has done so much for his country in the last forty years as George Norris.
> —William Allen White, Emporia, Kan.

Here is one from labor:

Unfortunately, the great work that men do in life is very often forgotten; but when the history of men in public life in recent years is written I am sure that the name and work of George Norris will stand out prominently because of his great efforts to be helpful, not only to all of the people of our country but especially to the workers, the toilers, the masses that need friends.

—Daniel J. Tobin, Indianapolis, Ind.

Here is one from the far West:

To me, one of the rarest privileges in connection with my Senate service was the opportunity of knowing and associating with George W. Norris. I think we all knew and recognized that he was the real statesman in the Senate. His long service resulted in more constructive accomplishments than that of any other member of the body.

—Lewis B. Schwellenbach, Spokane, Wash.

And here is one from his own state:

His Nebraska friends honor and love him in defeat as well as victory.

—J. E. Lawrence, Lincoln, Nebr.

Applause was renewed with each note.

Next, Justice Hugo L. Black stood before the senator and his distinguished friends.

"Men can continue to live in two ways," Justice Black opened. "One is through the work which they have actually accomplished. Another is through the work done by others, inspired by the spirit of the one who has gone. Measured by either of those tests, when the time arrives—which we hope will be many, many years in the future—men will know that George Norris continues to live."

Pounding hands rallied behind Black's words.

The stern justice pulled a long sheet of paper from his belongings and said, "Allow me to read a few remarks by promising young men about the senator." One twenty-eight-year-old attorney said Norris "symbolizes for me, as he must for all other young men in government, an ideal of public service."

Next Black read from a young college professor. The schoolman wrote: "What Senator Norris has done means more than the measure he has sponsored, more than the lasting blessings even of TVA. It means that inertia can be overcome, that transforming thought can ultimately prevail, that public work can be directed to great and domestic ends, and that what is needed to bring this about is warmth of heart, nobility of spirit, honesty of purpose, and a life of unremitting toil."

A young government worker had this to say: "There is a bond that unites Senator Norris and the young people of this country, a bond that is more durable than political union or geographical ties."

With a thoughtful grin, Black told of another young man, whom Senator Norris does not know, but who knows him. According to the speaker, the impressed young gentleman said: "I met Senator Norris once. He would not remember it—a random handshake and a few words—but I shall remember it for the rest of my life. Each of us has our own selection of American heroes—men of vision, principle and accomplishments. For me, Senator Norris stands foremost among that group of Americans. There are many young men who will be consciously following the leadership of his example long after he retires from government."

Emotional applause drowned out the speaker.

Now Justice Black recalled his earlier impressions of the Nebraskan. "It was in 1927 that I came from Alabama to Washington to become a member of the Senate. My ideas of Senator Norris were not then what my ideas are now. At the time Senator Norris did not have a high standing in the State of Alabama. As a matter of fact, before coming to Washington, I do not recall that I read anything that expressed any keen favor for the senator or his record, except what I had happened to see in a newspaper called 'Labor.'"

Shaking his head, the speaker added: "I had no remote idea, from that distance, that Senator Norris had influence in the Senate."

Black continued: "So far as I could tell, he was not the destructive character that my Alabamians had been caused to believe." He smiled. The honored guest smiled, too. To the pleasure of his audience, Black called Senator Norris "the most influential individual in the Senate."

The justice now turned to the election defeat of the senator. "You and I know, as all thinking people of America know, that it was not George Norris who was defeated. It was the people of Nebraska. They could not defeat him. He cannot be defeated. He is a symbol. He is a symbol of complete integrity—integrity of purpose, integrity of mind, and integrity of action."

Justice Black took his seat.

Vice President Henry Wallace stepped to the rostrum to pay tribute to "the best loved progressive of our time. He belongs to that small group of wise public men who clearly see the future and are willing to do something about it. They know that without progress there will be either revolution or the return of the human spirit to the cave."

The vice president went on to say:

Out of his trials came the ability to serve the common man. As a small boy, Senator Norris was forced by hard circumstance to think of others, because he lost his father and had to help support his mother. Thus he learned with his own hands the difficulties which tens of millions of our people face.

He thought things out for himself, slowly and carefully.

Events once in a long while proved that he was wrong, but when he found that to be the case, he was humble enough to change. It is a rare man who can grow, especially after he passes fifty years of age.

Wallace said that Norris understands the importance of conserving soil, water, electricity, and people. "And, he has done something about it," the speaker contended, citing the senator's role in instituting TVA and REA.

The vice president suggested that Norris showed this same broad vision in his support of the national farm program. The farm program, according to Wallace, meant conservation of soil and water and conservation of farm families and farm homes. "Why is it that Senator Norris, speaking softly and without oratorical effect, universally commands attention in the Senate when he takes the floor?" asked the vice president.

He quickly answered his own question: "It is because of his rare ability to make the most complicated issue seem clear and simple. He always talks the language of the average man."

Wallace told the audience he understood the people of the Tennessee Valley had asked Norris to make his home there, so that he could see his TVA dream become reality: "But, great as is the pull of the Tennessee mountains and valleys, the pull of the Nebraska prairies is greater. Senator Norris is going back to be among his old friends in McCook."

Suddenly, Wallace's voice boomed a decisive: "We don't want him to go. The progressive cause needs him," he emphasized.

"With George Norris' help and counsel the liberals of this nation can do their part in the hard, practical political job of making the world more secure for the common man of all the nations."

Now, it was Governor Matthew M. Neely of West Virginia doing the honors. "Never mind, Senator Norris, before the next six years have elapsed the people of your state and my own state will be much sorrier than you and I," the governor and former senatorial colleague began.

He continued:

Words used in an attempt to portray the greatness of George Norris, to describe his essential goodness, or to appraise the value of his services become as sounding brass and a tinkling cymbal. There are some events and a few personalities which simply defy portrayal by any language known to the human race.

Thomas Jefferson, Abraham Lincoln, William Jennings Bryan, Bob La Follette, Woodrow Wilson, Franklin D. Roosevelt, and George Norris constitute the most brilliant stars in the brightest constellation of humanitarian statesmen that ever has or ever will illumine the pages of American history.

Governor Neely recalled that "there has not been a single national battle for a humanitarian ideal in which George Norris has not been in the front-line trenches. During his entire lifetime, he has fought the battles of the common people." The governor declared: "The people here do not want you to go back to your loved ones in Nebraska. Something tells me that you are by no means at or near the end of the trail." Peering at Norris, his old colleague said: "Remember this, Cato learned Greek at eighty."

Paraphrasing, Neely concluded: "Here's to you, beloved statesman, patriot, public servant, and friend. May you live a thousand years, just to keep things progressive in this vale of human tears. May I live a thousand, too—no, a thousand less a day; for I should not want to be on earth to hear that you had passed away."

Senator Alben W. Barkley of Kentucky was at the rostrum. Norris, he began, is "a man who has come up from the ranks of the people and has never gotten beyond them or above them." The senator's record of achievement over the past four decades "shows that he has never yielded, never gone off on a side track, even for a moment, in his belief that government grows, that it must grow, and that whenever it ceases to grow society will be come static," Barkley continued. "No man in the history of this nation has given more of his energy, thought and character to the growth of government than has Sen. George Norris."

Turning to the center of the head table, the Kentucky lawmaker concluded:

Sen. Norris, you have been a little more patient than most of us who have wanted to move forward sometimes faster than the people were ready to travel.

You have had a little more charity for all than many of us, if not most of us. You have had a little more devotion to the liberal and progressive ideal than any of us.

You have a little more love. You have bowed down less to the past. You have been silent sometimes in ignoring pretended authority.

You have looked bravely forward to the future with faith in your fellowmen; and, because of this and your contribution to this great cause, your race, our race—all races—are tonight riper for a burst of light and life.

Toastmaster Hugo Black returned to the microphone. "If there ever was a time—and there was such a time—when the name of Sen. Norris was not spoken of with peculiar favor in the State of

1. The grave of George W. Norris in McCook, Nebraska. Nebraska State Historical Society (RG3298 PH4-10).

2. (*opposite top*) The Norris family home in McCook. George and Ellie moved into the house in 1899 but remodeled it extensively in 1932. George called it his little "PWA project in his own home town." Nebraska State Historical Society (RG3298 PH21-4).

3. (*opposite bottom*) Senator George W. Norris at the building of one of the Tennessee Valley Authority dams. Nebraska State Historical Society (RG3298 PH38-1).

4. (*above*) Norris at his cabin near Waupaca, Wisconsin, on Chain O'Lakes. Nebraska State Historical Society (RG3298 PH21-28).

5. (*opposite top*) A family photo of George and Ellie Norris with their three daughters, their husbands, and their children. Back row: Harold Nelson, Hazel Robertson, Jeanne DeWitt Nelson, John Robertson, Gertrude Rath, Marion Nelson, and Gordon Rath. Front row: Gretchen Rath, Ellie Norris, George Norris Rath, Senator George Norris, and Virginia Ann Nelson. Nebraska State Historical Society (RG3298 PH12-1).

6. (*opposite bottom*) Norris speaking to a crowd. Nebraska State Historical Society (RG3298 PH24-3).

7. (*above*) Tennessee Valley Authority committee member R. T. Hutchinson, Rural Electric Association administrator Harry Slattery, Norris, and National Rural Electric Cooperative Association president Steve Tate at the National Rural Electric Convention in St. Louis on January 19, 1943. Nebraska State Historical Society (RG3298 PH23-3).

8. Senator and Mrs. Norris getting off the Zephyr in McCook, Nebraska, January 22, 1943. Nebraska State Historical Society (RG3298 PH 19-1).

9. George and Ellie relaxing on the porch after his retirement from Congress. Nebraska State Historical Society (RG3298 PH7-1).

10. Norris in his sun room at home in McCook. Nebraska State Historical Society (RG3298 PH7-7).

11. Sculptor Jo Davidson working on the bust of Senator George W.
Norris. Nebraska State Historical Society (RG3298 PH 12-1).

Alabama, that time has passed. I believe there is no state among all the forty-eight states in which there would be a more nearly unanimous sentiment expressed against his withdrawal from public life than in the State of Alabama."

Black eyed Norris, and continued: "Of course, we do not want him to withdraw from public life. We know that McCook is calling him. However, he can go to McCook when he becomes old enough to retire." Kind laughter filled the room. "When he reaches the age of ninety-five, perhaps it would be all right for him to go back there. The people of the country are not yet willing to lose his services; and as one citizen of this nation, I wish to express the sincere hope that he will not find the lure of McCook so overpowering that he will permit himself to depart from public service. We need him. We must have him."

Applause rose like gunfire.

Black continued: "If he comes to the Tennessee Valley, where he probably will come, at least for a visit, if not for permanent residence, he will find that the people of that state still read a book which says that 'A good name is rather to be chosen than great riches, and loving favor rather than silver and gold.' I cannot think of anything that would be more appropriate in the history of this nation than for the man who dreamed the dream and saw the vision long before it came into reality to sit down and watch the splendor of that dream come true."

Justice Black's voice grew solemn. He now spoke softly. "If I were to introduce the President of the United States, I should do so with these words: 'The President of the United States.' Such a brief introduction, in my judgment, is always imperatively called for when one introduces a man who equals in stature the type of man who is the President of the United States. Gentlemen, the senator from Nebraska."

Suddenly, the crowd of luminaries was on its feet. Norris

worked his way through a maze of smiling faces and outstretched hands to the microphone. He carried no notes, but he had something very important to say.

First, an expression of fundamental belief: "The man who is happy only when he thinks of gains and disregards the sufferings of millions of others just as good as he is, has not yet learned the divine lesson which was taught centuries ago by the lowly Nazarene."

As always, his thoughts turned to the peace that surely must follow this bloody and brutal world conflict:

> It seems to me that all should realize, from the progress that has been made in this war so far, that we must have a new world, a new civilization, in order to make any success out of our victory.
>
> There must be a permanent peace, in which the individual, as well as nations all over the civilized world, will have the right to enjoy happiness and be free from the fear of poverty, death, and destruction, from the cradle to the grave.
>
> They must be free from misfortunes which they have had no hand in bringing about. It seems to me that the man who does not realize that clearly does not comprehend the present situation of the world.

Moving swiftly, Norris settled on TVA:

> Those who would attempt to destroy it would take away from our people the comfort and happiness which will come to us if we will only take care of our natural resources which God has given us.
>
> That is all TVA is. It merely utilizes, for the benefit of man—for the benefit of all of us—the proper conservation of nature's resources.

They ought to belong to all the people, instead of to a few. It is because of the few, powerful as they are, and influential as they are in elections, from road overseer to President, that we have had this constant struggle in the development of our natural resources.

Now, he had words for an old enemy: "So, I hope the National Association of Manufacturers will realize that while we may not be expected to build a TVA on the Danube, we ought to build one on the Missouri River and on the Mississippi River. We ought to build one in Arkansas. We ought to take advantage of all the water which flows from the mountains down to the sea, the power from which, if properly developed, would bring happiness to the American people, without enriching those who do not labor but only reap a reward from the labor of others."

A word of summation: "The resources which God has given to man should be developed by man for the benefit of man."

What is the TVA dream? "In a nutshell, it is to develop a stream. The same thing can be applied to every stream that comes down from the mountains."

Now, Norris reached for his closing: "To sum it all up, in order to have a satisfactory condition in the world, we must have a world peace in which no grief shall gnaw a heart, and never shall a tender tie be broken, and the eternal change that waits on growth and action shall proceed with everlasting accord, hand in hand."

Washington sounded its final farewell.

Nine

Norris had just settled into his rocker with a favorite book when the clatter from downstairs disturbed him. The shuffling of boxes and trunks grew increasingly loud, and the senator impatiently put down his book.

Up from the rocker, he headed for the basement door, but before he reached the entrance, the door swung open. Ellie had a pin in her hand. With a smile, she handed it to George William. He scanned the maroon and gold emblem with fond care. It was for him a symbol of his youth—and much more. It was loyalty and friendship and enduring camaraderie.

Norris returned to the chair. He held the pin under the sunlight. Worn little by age, the letters LUN shone in the morning sunshine. It has been some sixty-one years ago at Valparaiso University in Indiana that LUN had been born. Norris had lost a campus election by a single vote, and his supporters banded together behind him to form a new fraternal organization whose only secret was its name.

About a dozen members were included. No additional persons were ever to enter the closed society. They drew their own constitution, and pledged to meet once a year for the rest of their lives. The pledge was kept for fifty-nine years.

All members chipped in equal amounts to cover the expenses

of travel and lodging, and LUN convened every year, usually at a lake resort in Wisconsin, Iowa, Illinois, or Indiana. They printed programs of their activities, held a special banquet on Saturday night, and named a toastmaster and speakers. Sunday mornings they would meet on the porch of one of the cottages, hear the report of their treasurer, and elect new officers.

LUN was composed of lifelong friends, some lawyers and bankers, some judges and railroad men, one a senator. They usually met in August. Often in later years Point Comfort was the convention site. Two of Norris's Wisconsin lakeland neighbors were LUN associates. Sometimes the wives were along; sometimes they were not. In any event, the women never learned the secret of LUN, and they weren't allowed near the meeting sites. Often the wives would try to sneak up on the business sessions, but they were never successful.

At college, LUN's opponents had dubbed the fraternity "Lunatics Under Norris." Ellie always thought it might mean "loyalty-union-nobility."

Each member was assigned a topic, usually humorous, for the banquet session. It wasn't so long ago, Norris recalled, that he had stood before his friends and recited: "I look around me and I see friends of my youth grown old like me." Or the time he wrote this poem:

Of all the joys that life can bring,
The baby is the best,
I've learned to laugh and cry and sing,
And miss at night my rest.
And when at night from heavenly dreams,
I'm brought to earth a spell,
It's all because I think, it seems,
I've heard the baby yell.

To music of inferior brand,
All clothed in robes of white,
With baby in supreme command,
I march the floor at night.
But when those little eyelids close,
In slumber peaceful sweet,
I kneel beside my slumbering rose
And kiss her on the cheek.
And kneeling there, in accents mild,
I send up thanks to God,
And ask Him to protect my child,
When I'm beneath the sod.
Then fill the flowing goblets well,
And drink with joy serene,
To her whose charms I love to tell,
My pride, my love, my queen.

These words, Norris thought, were appropriate for Hazel, who traveled faithfully by his side through thick and thin. She has been a constant joy and a beacon of light, he assured himself.

He recalled that the simple but sincere lines were written at the first LUN reunion after Hazel was born. It was titled "The Responsibility of Parenthood."

LUN had not only made Norris a better man, but it also contributed to his growth as a representative of the people, he told himself many times. Through the years of correspondence with his old college associates, Norris kept a closer check on the public pulse. Each associate took a special interest in his region and in turn kept the senator posted. Norris referred to their written bits of information as "a faithful picture of Americans' march." With pride, Norris often spoke of his LUN brothers and their respective accomplishments in life. A truly remarkable group, he thought.

Chuckling, Norris recalled the short poem he had authored for the 1927 reunion at Rainbow Lake:

Once there was a lazy boy who ran away from school.
The LUN took after him and ducked him in a pool;
They quenched his thirst with castor oil, put pepper in his eyes,
Then filled his mouth with angleworms, and made him eat
    some flies.
They took him to the woods and tied him to a log,
They cut him up in pieces and fed him to a hog.
So you better do your duty and be kind to all about,
Or the LUN will get you if you don't watch out.

The organization had originated with a banquet in the Merchants' Hotel at Valparaiso on August 6, 1883. As "chief worthy," Norris presided at the first affair. The 1884 meeting was again at Valparaiso. Later, LUN moved to the lakes, including Okoboji in Iowa and Lake Delavan and Brown's Lake in Wisconsin. The Grand View Hotel overlooking Rainbow Lake finally became LUN's permanent home.

As death cut the ranks, the meetings became more solemn. The fifty-ninth banquet was held at Haleiwa on August 30, 1941. Finally, the membership dropped to two. Norris became chief worthy and Ermon E. Smith of Dodge City, Kansas, was vice-worthy. The 1941 reunion was LUN's last.

LUN was many things to George Norris. It was a firm expression of lasting friendship, a unique example of lifelong association. A solid bond held these men together more than six decades. Only death could separate them—and old age.

Two were living today, but a combination of age and war had broken the long string of reunions in 1942. LUN would never meet again, Norris realized.

Its last meeting attracted the final three survivors. Each held an office; each spoke at the banquet; a program was printed; the treasurer's report was read; one had served as toastmaster.

Now, Norris understood, LUN was a thing of the past, a precious, dear, and cherished memory. As George Norris fingered his pin, it was not pain or sorrow that filled his heart. It was the pleasure of the past, a sweet memory of earlier days. LUN was a joy to recall, one of the happiest associations of a long and active life.

Ten

Senator Robert Crosby, the young Speaker of the 1943 Nebraska Unicameral Legislature, intently studied the face of the white-haired man who was marching up the aisle toward him.

He looks like a man in his late sixties, Crosby thought to himself. He bears himself with dignity; he seems to be quite composed; and he appears extremely senatorial, the North Platte legislator was thinking.

The galleries had risen in a standing ovation, and the warmth and noise of this greeting far surpassed anything Crosby had ever heard in the austere and dignified West Senate Chambers. The legislative committee of five turned with their guest as he reached the front of the podium, and accompanied him up the three steps that led to the platform.

Crosby leaned over, shook hands, and greeted Senator George W. Norris on his first visit to the unique unicameral legislature that he had fathered.

The aged warrior stood at the west end of the room and faced the large crowd that nearly overflowed the great marble and stone chamber. Above him on either side and far across the enclosure at its east end, the wooden balcony benches were hidden by the standing observers. As the senator looked up at them, his eyes settled for a moment on the six shining chandeliers that were suspended from the high, beamed ceiling.

People filled chairs below on both sides behind the eighteen splendid ornate Gothic columns that separated the gallery from the Senate floor. Directly in front of him, senators were on their feet beside the deep-cushioned swivel chairs from which they conduct their business. Behind them, in the rear seats, were the lobbyists and special guests of the legislature. Back there too stood Jim Lawrence, who had accompanied Norris to the skyscraper statehouse this day.

Norris nodded to the demonstrative audience, and they began to take their seats.

Crosby stepped forward toward the microphone. So, at last he had come, Crosby thought to himself as he moved near the stand. Over his left shoulder the calendar read March 10. The invitation had been extended by legislative resolution on January 19.

A dramatic moment. The eighty-two-year-old legislative giant, beaten just four months ago in a bitter, heartbreaking defeat, had journeyed the 225 miles from McCook to Lincoln in the twilight of his life to view what he had created. A sentimental journey; a pilgrimage to the seat of Nebraska state government.

Crosby had met the senator before only long enough to shake hands. He had anxiously awaited this opportunity to view him at close range. A young man with ambition, Bob Crosby would never forget this moment. Many years later, he could recall the scene clearly.

"This is a unique situation in the strict sense of the word," Crosby began. We have had speakers and expect to have more in the future. But none will be more significant. George W. Norris is far beyond any other living Nebraskan in shaping the history of the state, the nation and the world. We feel humble as he comes before us today."

To a new and generous round of applause, Norris approached the rostrum.

In the back of the chamber, Jim Lawrence was now recalling how it had all come about. It had been a hot and dusty summer back in 1934. As editor of the *Lincoln Star*, Lawrence had watched carefully the senator's one-man campaign to enact a constitutional amendment creating the Unicameral.

It began in Hastings, a hundred miles west of Lincoln. From there, in a bid to convince Nebraskans of the advantages of a one-house legislature, Norris traveled dusty mile after mile, day after day across the great open expanse of the state.

With John Robertson at his side, they drove on against the combined force of both political parties and the weather. Their car's fenders were stripped of paint by the blinding dust and gravel. The windshield became so pitted at one time that one could barely see through it. West of O'Neill in north-central Nebraska, a terrifying dust storm halted them only temporarily. South of Lincoln—with the wind howling and the dust swirling about in hazy columns—Norris spoke from atop the tailgate of a wagon. It had been that way all across the breadth of this parched prairie state, from the Missouri River in the east to the Sandhills of the northwest. Norris spoke where he could, and he had a hunch the people were listening.

The senator pounded away at the theme that a two-house legislature is too often controlled by its small conference committees and they, in turn, are easily swayed by lobbyists. Too much good legislation dies in the conference room or is torn to bits in an effort to please both houses and the pressure groups, Norris told his listeners.

In a one-house system, there is no conference committee. It would be easier to pin responsibility directly on the elected lawmakers. They could not hide in the conference room or blame the pressures of the other house. It was clearly a matter of fishing or cutting bait, Norris noted.

Mile after mile, Norris and Robertson carried the message. A legislature is like a board of directors in a large corporation, the senator pointed out. Thus, there is need for only one house.

Norris insisted that the Unicameral be nonpartisan. Where some of its supporters were willing to scrap this feature in order to melt some of the opposition, the senator was unwilling to yield. He stood fast, arguing that the nonpartisan aspect must be retained. It was.

Both political parties threw heavy opposition in the path of the constitutional proposal. The *Omaha World-Herald* added its loud and influential voice. Jim Lawrence proudly recalled that his newspaper had backed Norris and the Unicameral.

The people of Nebraska adopted the one-house legislative system in the fall of 1934. The Unicameral opened its first session in 1937.

Now, in its fourth session, Norris had come to see the system at work. Lawrence looked across the chamber to the great high arch of muraled stone under which the senator stood. The clock over his shoulder indicated that it would soon be noon. Portraits of Washington and Lincoln flanked him on the wall behind. Farther to the sides stood the Stars and Stripes and the flag of Nebraska.

How fitting, the Lincoln editor thought. Few men could stand comfortably in the shadow of Washington and Lincoln, but Norris seemed not at all out of place there, Lawrence decided. And it was proper that the flags of the governments he had served for a lifetime were to look upon this historic moment.

Crosby stared at the senator. The cordial reception that had been accorded Norris still echoed in the Speaker's ears. It had been unusual applause, a hearty welcome for a senior statesman whose record was now, at the least, controversial.

Crosby decided one thing for sure: this was indeed a great man, a man of tremendous stature. His demeanor was dignified. He was gracious and composed. Crosby thought he looked well physically, certainly not eighty—or even seventy. He was vigorous, and he spoke with clarity and force, the young North Platte legislator observed.

As Crosby listened, Norris spoke of the history of the Unicameral, how it had proven successful in comparison to bicameral bodies. "The world will pass on this system by what you do, not so much as the laws you may enact, but as to your preservation of every democratic right all free people should have," the senator's voice rang.

Scanning the varied expressions before him, Norris continued: "What little part I had in bringing this legislature about, is a part of my life in which I always take satisfaction and pride."

Moving along quickly with his extemporaneous message, the renowned visitor noted that the benefits of the Unicameral have not yet been fully realized. "When we brush the cobwebs of prejudice from our brains, we will see and realize the important step that was taken in human progress," he declared forcefully. Applause broke through.

Next, the senator pointed to objections raised against the one-house legislative system as "being more easily influenced or controlled by lobbyists and that it didn't provide the check and balance system enjoyed by bicameral legislatures." Clearing his throat with a drink of water, Norris lambasted both arguments: "Those who have been critical forget that government never will be free of the lobby. There is a tendency to forget the lobby that howls around the other legislatures. But, I'd like to see the Nebraska Unicameral like Caesar's wife—above suspicion. All parliamentary bodies ought to protect themselves against paid lobbyists, representing big corporations, special interests who work for legislation which favors them. I have heard that lobbyists have come right on the floor of the Unicameral, but if that is true, then you should correct it."

Turning his verbal attack on the check and balance criticism, Norris thundered: "The very existence of the Unicameral demonstrates such isn't true."

Then with a broad grin, he added: "At the end of any 'two-barrelled' legislature I ever knew about, the lobby had the checks and the special interests had the balances."

Now the senator moved into a discussion of how the Unicameral came about. "I had only one motive in its creation. That was to improve conditions. And I think we've done it," he remarked. "There is only one change that I would suggest—that would be to increase your salaries. At the time the one-house system was discussed, I suggested even a smaller body with larger salaries. You ought to have a salary which would enable you to give your full time to the study of the government in Nebraska."

Norris recalled that the nonpartisan feature of the unicameral proposal provided one of the hottest controversies when the committee went to work to draw up the constitutional amendment providing for the one-house system. "I stood alone on the nonpartisan feature," he said. "Politics is a sore to any government. It is one of the greatest hindrances that exists to good government. Any man must be condemned when he puts his party ahead of his country. Partisanship, if carried to the extreme, will ruin everything." But, Norris noted, "I found out people don't care whether you are Republican or Democrat. They want to know what you represent."

Norris discussed the Unicameral's rules, its mandatory requirement that a public hearing be held on every bill. His tone continued in a congratulatory vein to Nebraska lawmakers for having carried forward the spirit of the Unicameral along the lines he had intended.

There was no reference at all to his future, Crosby carefully observed. The press had toyed with a rumor that Norris might seek a seat in the legislature, but Crosby doubted it. In the east end of the chamber, Jim Lawrence also doubted it. The senator, Lawrence recalled, had told him his public service had ended. He had said it in a letter a day after his defeat. He had repeated it to him today on the way to the statehouse.

It was hard to imagine George Norris as a state senator after his forty years in Washington, the last three decades a member of the most powerful legislative body on earth. And Norris had been during the last decade or more one of the most influential men in the nation.

Lawrence thought of Norris with Roosevelt, how they had worked hand in hand to accomplish what both of them believed needed to be done for the nation. He knew that Nebraskans had not always agreed, but until the previous fall they had trusted Norris enough to allow him to continue to make the decisions for them in Washington. So it was that Lawrence suddenly shook his head, flicking off the last lingering doubt that Norris might consent to seek a legislative seat after all.

In McCook, Ellie wondered how it was all going for George William in Lincoln. She glanced at the clock. It was noon. Surely, he would be finished speaking by now, she thought, probably on his way to lunch with Jim Lawrence.

Ellie had remained behind this trip. The weather in Nebraska in March is unpredictable, and besides, George William appeared in good spirits and would not need her along. Nevertheless, she would be glad when he returned. Ellie didn't like to see George William make these long trips. She rested easier when he was at home.

As his eye began to wander, Norris recognized many spectators from past associations, but an equally large number of them were strangers. How odd, and yet gratifying, it was to have people he didn't know applauding. Yet, it was even more strange to the senator to realize that many of his constituents from the early unicameral days were absent—absent because of politics.

Norris and his once beloved Republican Party had fallen out over a series of issues. The party bigwigs violently opposed his open support of Democrat Al Smith for the presidency in 1928; they opposed his theory of public ownership in the Tennessee Valley; they came to generally oppose his liberal leanings; and finally, they took sides against his plan for a one-house, nonpartisan legislature.

In 1936 the not-to-be-bullied senator from McCook sought reelection as an Independent, rather than a Republican. He won. The party was bitter. This bitterness, Norris full well realized, remained intense even to this cold March day.

Norris still liked, respected, and tried to keep contact with many of the old party leaders, but he was not one to bend—especially on a political issue. Their bitterness made the senator even more fervent in his desire for nonpartisanship in government. It was his firm insistence on the omission of partisan politics from the Unicameral that dealt the crowning blow to the Republican leaders. They openly fought his nonpartisan legislature.

Scattered about the galleries were rural Nebraska power representatives, in Lincoln for the convention of the Nebraska Association of Rural Public Power Districts. They would hear Norris this night at their dinner meeting. Some in the know had already been told that the senator might take after controversial Legislative Bill 204, a private power measure that Norris considered "disgraceful."

Members of the legislature were to be the association's guests that night, so they would have a second opportunity to consider the senator's views.

Outside the chamber door, in the spacious and breathtaking second floor statehouse rotunda, visitors could hear Norris's voice as it spilled out into the great structure. People turned to step quickly across the minutely tiled floor to the padded high door beyond which the senator spoke. They paused at the cushioned railing and listened.

Lobbyists seated in the rear rows of the senate floor heard the senator warn of their power. Only they wondered if these special interest representatives of whom Norris spoke really meant them. Must be the fellow across the aisle, each decided with a sidelong glance at his associates.

Near the front of the chamber in the side balconies, a number of school-age children leaned over the high ledge to catch a better view of the man their parents and teachers had spoken of. My, he did look important, they thought.

Here and there, across the room, a bright ambitious young man envisioned himself years hence returning to the legislature from his place of high position to address his fellow Nebraskans on a similarly auspicious occasion.

In small groups stood a number of state employees, neatly divided into their respective offices. Secretaries on coffee breaks, those who had left early for lunch and some who had gained permission from the boss to have a look at the senator listened.

Newspaper reporters frantically tried to catch nearly every word. With no text available, the task was that much more difficult. This story was worth recording in full.

The cluttered desks of the lawmakers themselves remained untouched during the short address. The morning papers sat unnoticed on the broad wooden counters. Copies of Nebraska statutes lined the front of the desks. Bills lay in odd piles near the drawers. Unsigned letters had to wait. Cups of water grew warm. Conversation between members had ceased.

63

Before closing, Norris gave his listeners a look at the raging war picture: "The American people have yet to reach the point where we are unanimous in unity behind the government and its allies. There are objectives to everything that is done. Then, the peace that comes must be everlasting. It is as important as the war."

Crosby leaned forward as he sensed the final remarks. He would always cherish the picture of himself with Norris taken on the platform that morning. A decade later, it was to remain one of his prize mementos when he became governor.

With a final expression of gratitude, Norris bade the legislature farewell. Crosby was on his feet. The clock on the wall stood at 12:10 p.m.

Eleven

Why?

Jim Lawrence would attempt to answer the question eloquently framed in the eyes of George Norris. The senator did not need to ask. As he settled into a chair in the editor's second-floor, north-east-corner office, Norris was ready to listen. He lit a fresh cigar, and Lawrence began to talk.

They had returned not long before from lunch following the appearance at the Unicameral. Now the two men were to review, through Lawrence's soft words, the campaign of 1942. Lawrence had been the senator's campaign manager, having headed a peti-tion drive that placed Norris on the ballot as an independent can-didate. The senator had early that year decided not to seek a sixth term, but some of his supporters would not hear of it. At last, in September, Norris accepted their petition plea.

Republican Kenneth Wherry and Democrat Foster May were already in the race, so it would be another difficult three-man contest. There had been one in 1936 too, and Norris had won as an independent.

While Wherry and May canvassed the state during the fall months, Norris remained on the job in Washington. It wasn't until October 29 that he entered his home state. The election was five days off.

It was just after midnight when his train pulled into Lincoln. Norris was all smiles. The train was two hours late, but Lawrence had waited patiently at the station. The two friends plotted campaign strategy at the Cornhusker Hotel before the senator retired for the night.

Plans were announced for a speech that next evening in the Cornhusker ballroom at 8 p.m. The senator was to speak in Omaha Saturday night, then in Grand Island Sunday. Addresses at Kearney and Hastings on Monday would conclude the whirlwind campaign.

In Lincoln, Norris spoke before an overflow crowd, pointing to his experience and citing his record of forty years' service. The speech was heavily laced with disdain for partisan politics, particularly in a time of war.

In Omaha the next night, Norris outlined a plan for peace. It involved the stationing of a compact army of occupation in each of the defeated Axis nations. It revolved about the prevention of rearmament and a complete embargo on the construction of war production facilities. Total disarmament was its key.

Then, he turned to the harsh politics of this campaign. Norris had been accused of me-tooism and blind allegiance to Roosevelt. "Frankly, I say to you now that if you expect me to follow any President when I think he is wrong, or if you expect me to jump at the crack of the party whip, you had better put someone else in my place," he replied. "I will not be that kind of a hired man or rubber stamp."

He lashed Wherry for charging that the Roosevelt administration was keeping General MacArthur out of Guadalcanal for partisan motives, fearing it would aid MacArthur's chances as a possible Republican presidential candidate. Spreading such rumors, Norris declared, was nothing short of accusing the President of disloyalty.

Altogether, the senator made eight talks in four days in five cities.

Support for his candidacy came from the pen of Jim Lawrence. Writing in the editorial columns of the *Star*, Lawrence termed his opponents' argument that Norris is too old "absurd." The *Star* urged reelection of "the unterrified warrior who raises his shield and sword in defense of the underprivileged." Washington newspaper correspondents and columnists bought an ad in Nebraska publications urging reelection of the old warrior.

Norris's own ad—"written and paid for by the Norris for Senator Committee"—screamed the slogan: "Mid-stream is no place to change hosses." Noting the values of experience and the danger of change especially during time and war, it argued: "A useful, powerful, influential member of the U.S. Senate does not emerge overnight—in seven days—nor a year. Long experience does count in times of deadly peril. When terribly sick, you send for the best doctor or best surgeon."

Of Norris, it read: "He has never failed you. You have taken your troubles to him—your troubles, both large and small—and out of his decent purpose and his long experience, he has helped you solve them."

It continued:

> He is needed in this war.
> He has one master—and that is his true conscience.
> He is needed for the peace which will follow.
> He is needed for that peace to write into it a purpose for history's tomorrow as well as history's today.

Then, moving to counteract the great danger a united Republican Party might present to the senator's candidacy, it pleaded: "Forget party politics. Keep Nebraska's great liberal, George W. Norris, on the job." The senator was pictured at the side of the ad, and it concluded with a suggestion to listen to the radio in the final days of the campaign.

On Monday November 2, the day before the election, a United Press dispatch from Omaha summed up the prospects. "It's a 4-to-5 and take your choice with the Omaha betting fraternity," Tom W. Ingoldsby wrote. Norris and Wherry were headed toward "possibly a photo finish."

That night, Norris was en route to Washington by train. It was drizzling in McCook, with a smattering of snow. Nebraskans had made their decision, and the only task remaining was a tabulation of their votes. In newsrooms throughout the state, early returns gave a clear indication of the final result. Lawrence moved sadly to his typewriter. In Omaha, Ingoldsby worked on his lead.

Editors were alerted throughout the nation that big news was coming out of Nebraska that night. They clamored for the latest returns and dug in their files for background on the veteran senator.

On the train, Norris was asleep.

Ingoldsby handed his lead to the teletype operator, and machines began to chatter throughout the country. "One of the most outstanding men ever to grace the halls of the U.S. Senate ended his political career yesterday when the Nebraska electorate relegated Sen. George W. Norris to political oblivion," it read.

Lawrence looked at the editorial emerging from his typewriter: "His friends only will revere him more, and love him more . . . nor will they whine or moan."

Ingoldsby noted that Norris had carried into the race the blessings of Roosevelt. The President had endorsed his candidacy with the same statement he had issued in 1936.

Republicans had swept the state, and, in fact, appeared on their way to gaining forty seats in the House and ten Senate seats throughout the nation. Even the senator's native Red Willow

County had voted entirely Republican—except for county treasurer.

Norris had based his campaign on his record. Wherry had challenged the administration's conduct of the war, now in the dark days of late 1942. Many supporters had suggested that Norris's age made it doubtful that he could survive a sixth six-year term.

Nationally, wire services were rounding up the election results. Norris's defeat, one noted, was "symptomatic of a strong if scattered anti-administration trend."

Final tabulations for the day told the story: Wherry, 162,605; Norris, 91,732, and May, 74,441. Wherry had polled almost as many votes as Norris and May combined. Lawrence pointed to the GOP trend and dissatisfaction with the conduct of the war in explaining the senator's defeat.

Republican State Chairman A. T. "Bert" Howard of Scottsbluff was on the phone with a statement, the same one he had made September 28, the day Norris became a candidate. "It is unfortunate—there always comes a day when the champ goes down in defeat and that time has come in Nebraska politics," it read. "Never again will the Republican Party allow an independent candidate to divide its strength."

In Washington, unaware of the election results back home, Norris stepped off the train.

The scene was recorded by A. Shirley Brown of United Press:

Senator George W. Norris, defeated after forty years in the Congress, walked slowly from a railroad sleeping car into Washington's great Union Station at 7:23 a.m. today.

On his face, as he walked beside his daughter, Mrs. John P. Robertson, were lines of sadness which seemed to recall words he uttered about six weeks before the election.

"A defeat at this stage of the game, at my age," the

69

81-year-old statesman said then, "would be, in effect, a repudiation of all my life's work by the people whom I love."

Now the election was over and Norris had come back from his home state to serve out the remaining two months of his term. He was met by this reporter and his daughter, Hazel.

His eyes were moist; Norris spoke just five words:

"Well—there is no hope."

Norris could answer no questions. He had no statement for the press. He gripped this reporter's arm and dropped his eyes, as though to hide the emotion poorly concealed in them.

But, Norris, as he walked to a waiting automobile, did not have the appearance of a man who believed he had experienced anything but defeat.

The same day, Norris penned a letter to Lawrence:

Dear Jim,

I have just arrived in Washington and did not know the results of the election until I reached here.

It will always be a source of gratification and pride that we made an honorable and an honest fight and that we went down to defeat for reasons that even our enemies cannot explain.

This is the first campaign in my life where no fault was found by anyone, so far as I know, with my public record.

Of course, I do know that it is a personal repudiation of my life work . . .

It is the end of my public career. Although it is sad—bitterly sad—for me, yet I believe we were right.

My only hope is that after I am gone and forgotten, this philosophy will rise again. I have faith it will. It is true—it is eternal.

In McCook, the *Gazette* recalled the words of Norris in introducing Wherry before a gathering in 1929. The newspaper reprinted an editorial published November 20, 1931.

Norris had said: "Sen. Wherry is one of the most promising young statesmen to honor Nebraska, having served as an outstanding member in two sessions of the Nebraska Senate. He has demonstrated himself to be a forceful representative of the people's interests, a man of outstanding ability, always fighting for what he conscientiously believes to be right."

Having repeated Norris's words of thirteen years before, the *Gazette* took a deep breath and predicted that Wherry "will serve Nebraska with credit to himself and Nebraska." Then, outdoing itself, it added: "He will be the popular choice of the Republican Party for the vice presidency in 1944."

That was the way the end had come for Norris four months ago. Lawrence reviewed it gently, as an old friend. Norris said little, but he listened carefully now as the editor turned back to his editorial summation the week of the election. Norris had been beaten by a Republican wave and dissatisfaction with war—two factors, neither of which Norris had control over. His record had not been a genuine issue in the campaign.

So, Lawrence attempted to explain, his defeat had not really been a rejection of either the senator or his program, his life's work or his beliefs. Nebraskans had elected Republican nominees no matter who they were or what they stood for, Lawrence continued.

Norris nodded when the editor had finished. He was grateful to hear Lawrence's views and the rich praise he showered upon the senator's public record. But though he would not contradict Lawrence's conclusions aloud, he steadfastly maintained to himself that the defeat was a rejection of his program.

Surely, the people could have found his name on the ballot and parted with their Republican convictions just once. Surely, they knew that he was not responsible for the war or its conduct. Surely, if they had believed he was the right man and that his record merited their continued confidence, then they would have reelected him.

No, Norris would not argue with Lawrence's words. But neither would he accept them.

The conversation died as Norris fumbled through his pockets for a match to revive his black cigar. Lawrence took this opportunity to silently observe: the senator looks so very tired . . . and he moves with such careful deliberations . . . and he talks so softly. How strange it seemed to the Lincoln editor to view his old friend in this new and unhappy light. Lawrence could remember only the younger and happier days. His mind lived again with the memories of an enthusiastic statesman from Nebraska who was pounding out future legislative programs and possible remedies for pressing foreign ills.

Now, others were on stage and George Norris was in the audience. What a mighty weapon the people wield to wound such a giant, Lawrence decided.

Immediate members of the Norris family never talked of the somber November morning.

Now, more than ever, the Lincoln newspaperman wished that he could have greeted the senator in Washington that morning. He then would have tried to explain the returns in a comforting manner.

Lawrence clinched his fists and rapped his knuckles atop the cluttered desk.

Twelve

"Can the senator come outside, Mrs. Norris? I have something to show him."

There, at the front step of the Norris home, stood a shiny new tricycle. Its freckle-faced owner of five smiled toothlessly.

Ellie put a finger to her lips and explained that the senator was napping. But, she added with an understanding smile, George William would be up soon and quite anxious to see the new tricycle.

From the southeast bedroom window, a heavy-eyed, silver-haired observer smiled as the excited youngster peddled down the block toward home.

"He belongs to all of us," Ellie told her early morning coffee guest.

From atop the stairs, the words rang home to Norris, whose memory flashed back to the night of December 29, 1942.

"He belongs to all of us, and now, more than ever, all of us need his wise counsel and his inspiring leadership," Max Zaritsky, president of the United Hatters Cap and Millinery Workers Union (AFL) was saying.

The occasion: a testimonial dinner to Senator George W. Norris under the auspices of "The Nation" and the Union for Democratic Action. More than 1,500 persons had jammed the ballroom of the Hotel Commodore in New York City for the dinner that was to direct a plea to Norris to lead the liberal cause despite his defeat.

The observers had come to the crowded ballroom for many reasons. They wanted to see the man who had snapped the iron rule of the Speaker of the House. The Speaker at the time was "Uncle Joe" Cannon of Illinois, who had ruled the House as if it were his own private czardom. They wanted to see the man who had teamed up with New York Congressman Fiorello La Guardia to push the Norris–La Guardia Act of 1932. The so-called "yellow dog" contract was tossed out and rigid anti-injunction provisions were written into law.

Injunctions against labor had become a decisive weapon. Commenting on them, Senator Norris had said: "These injunctions have denied access to the courts. They have denied to the toiling masses the rights which are essential to human freedom. The tyranny of these injunctions, in their effect, reminds us of the days when slavery was recognized by the Constitution."

President Herbert Hoover signed the Norris–La Guardia measure only after its supporters had rounded up more than two-thirds of the members of each house, thereby making a veto appear ineffective.

They wanted to see the man who had vigorously instituted the Twentieth Amendment to the Constitution. This amendment changed the date of the inauguration of the President from March 4 to January 20, and thereby reduced the interim period between election and assumption of office. Such a change made it improbable that an outgoing or "lame duck" President might take arbitrary action while still in power. The Norris amendment became popularly known as the "Lame Duck Amendment."

They wanted to see the man who had wielded the foremost liberal voice in the days of Harding, Coolidge, and Hoover. They wanted to see the man whose work in Congress paved the way for the program of liberal legislation that was to come in the early days of the New Deal. They wanted to see the man who had protected unions in the National Industrial Recovery Act and was especially helpful to railroad unions in their legislative efforts.

They wanted to see the man who hated communism. The senator's opposition was not based on fear of communism, but rather upon hatred of the causes that aided in its development. In 1920 he said: "Communism does not breed in a country where the people are happy and satisfied. . . . Communism is born where labor is denied its just reward, and pressed down almost into human bondage. . . . The danger of dictatorship arises when the common people are unable to obtain justice under the laws and when those who toil on the farm, in the workshop, and in the counting houses, are overburdened and bowed down with injustice at the hands of those who control the property of the nation."

They wanted to see the man who with his own hands had harnessed a network of electricity for rural America through the creation of the REA. They wanted to see the man who had given hope to the peoples of the Tennessee Valley through the establishment of the TVA.

They wanted to see the man.

The program included such names as Mrs. Franklin D. Roosevelt; Senator Robert F. Wagner of New York; Fiorello H. La Guardia, now mayor of New York City; Will Rogers Jr., the young congressman-elect from California; Philip Murray, president of the Congress of Industrial Organizations; and James Patton, president of the National Farmers Union.

It was a night of historical speech making.

Mrs. Roosevelt set the pace: "Perhaps Providence has given us something which we hardly deserve. I never have felt that Senator Norris has been defeated. I always have felt that the people of this country have been defeated."

Murray, noting that he spoke for five million laboring men, was blunt. "I have come tonight, George, to plead with you, yes, to command you, come on, George and lead us," Murray declared. He proposed that Norris coordinate liberal and labor groups and "fight the kind of fight that we know you are capable of fighting." Labor, he said, "has a prime interest in winning this war. It has pledged itself to our great commander-in-chief. It has bled, wept, and died to win this war, but we want to make sure that in defeating the assurance of final victory in that direction, labor tonight is demanding that Senator Norris give to the people of the United States his service as our leader. Now labor looks toward George Norris again, a young man in splendid condition, ready to meet any adversaries. George Norris, we are ready to follow."

Young Rogers declared: "I am probably the only man on the platform who never had met Senator Norris, but I have felt his influence. Short story writers talk about the man who has influenced them. Well, Senator Norris has been my Hemingway."

Zaritsky, speaking for one of the larger AFL unions, then carried the ball: "He is not the mere representative of his native state. He is democracy's gift to all America. He belongs to all of us, and now, more than ever, all of us need his wise counsel and his inspiring leadership. And because he has shown how free men, through their own efforts, can maintain and enlarge the area of freedom, he had laid an obligation on all of us to carry on his battles—which are our battles—in his spirit. No matter how great the odds, we must carry on the struggle for a freer America—because George W. Norris has shown us that the odds do not matter, when the cause is just."

Patton said:

You, Senator Norris, never were more needed than now. In your own generation, there are millions of people who look to you. My generation also looks to you. It is a generation that has been through the wringer of postwar boom and bust, a few years of the New Deal and its submergence in the conversion to war.

We need a guide, a prophet, a counselor and a leader in this great crusade to save man's freedom on this earth. We have that man in George W. Norris, for however long it may please Providence to spare him for this work.

Respectively, humbly, but with the greatest earnestness and determination, on behalf of millions of men and women, I request and challenge him to undertake this final task of inspiration, organization, and leadership.

Senator Wagner picked up the tempo:

And so, as Senator Norris puts down the burden of office, the American people look to him to assume a far greater service—to exert his influence upon the thoughts and actions of free men the world over who wrestle with the problems of the peace.

I pray he may find it possible to remain in the forefront of public discussion, as a prophet with honor among all his fellows regardless of party, as a practical realist helping to keep our steps on the path he trod.

In the trials that lie ahead, may all of us prove worthy of his example, worthy of the blessings that God has showered upon our land, and worthy of the hopes of all humanity.

La Guardia urged: "The liberals and progressives should be gathered in given affirmative leadership. It would teach all of us prima donnas a little discipline which we need. Give the command and we will follow."

Supreme Court Justice William O. Douglas praised Norris:

When we speak of high character and integrity we mean more, of course, than simple honesty. We mean complete devotion to our way of life.

We mean the ideal of putting the office above the incumbent. We mean the use of the office not to gain power and privilege but to serve the people.

We mean that a national office has not been shrunk by the provincialism of the holder to the proportions of a local one.

We mean that the office-holder has not suffered his public responsibilities to be diluted by his private loyalties.

We mean an uncompromising devotion to the democratic ideal when the price of that devotion is slander and attack as well as when the rewards are high and the applause from the gallery resounds.

These are the reasons, in addition to the great causes he espoused, why Senator Norris occupies a high place in our American traditions.

They are the reasons why the inspiration of his outstanding public service will be a potent force in American life long after this generation has passed into history.

The dinner program that night carried "a call to action" from Freda Kirchwey, editor of *The Nation*. It read:

The defeat of George Norris in last November's elections will, I firmly believe, result in a period of new and broader service for him and in a spiritual awakening for the country.

Defeat is sometimes more salutary than victory, and the election in November should be looked upon as America's political Dunkirk—a shock which will rekindle the fighting faith of the progressive forces in this country.

On every ground—experience, valor in action, wisdom, even seniority—George Norris is the natural commander of those forces. His retirement from the Senate of the United States frees him for active field service in a war we know today must be fought on all fronts—from the farms of Nebraska to the shores of Tripoli.

The fight is for a world that belongs to the ordinary man to whom George Norris has devoted his strength, his integrity, his undiminished courage.

It will be a tough fight. The setback suffered by the democratic spirit in America is a real one. Our enemies are confident and aggressive.

We can win only if we accept defeat as a challenge, if we rouse ourselves to fight together and fight hard.

And this we are determined to do. Confidently, we summon George Norris to lead us in this greatest battle of all.

On the front cover of that program, the words of Franklin Delano Roosevelt were recalled. In describing Norris, he had said: "In our national history we have had few elder statesman who like him have preserved the aspirations of youth as they accumulated the wisdom of years. He is one of the major prophets of America."

Norris arose to a great ovation, a rousing roar that swept the Commodore's ballroom and carried into the hall outside. As always, his thoughts turned to what would follow the war: "The outcome of the present world war will determine whether we are to have a free world or whether a dictator shall make slaves of all the peoples of the earth who do not belong to his race. We will emerge from this contest a free people or we and our descendants will become the slaves of a master who knows neither justice nor mercy."

America's imperfections troubled him: "In this great world struggle, where the life of civilization is at stake, we will not be able to do our part in the drawing of the peace treaty unless we maintain the fires of human freedom at our own firesides. We must not be so illogical as to try to impose the principles of freedom upon other peoples if we are not practicing the same philosophy ourselves."

Progressive gains at home dare not be overlooked with the building of peace: "It is therefore essential that whatever advance we have made in progressive government in our own country shall be maintained with jealous care lest we lose the fruits of our advancement here in the reconstruction days which shall follow the war. The task will soon be before those who believe that they should rally around the banner of human progress to see that the gains we have made at home shall not be lost in the victory we shall win abroad."

Now, Norris had a warning: "The representatives of special interests already are attempting to frame the future so that, when the war is won and peace is made, they will be in control of a great part, if not all, of our governmental structure. Many of them are now in key positions, waiting for the time to come to act directly where they are now acting indirectly and in secret, in controlling our governmental policies."

Moving to counteract a force that might develop as a result of the bloody world conflict, Norris took the offensive:

Everyone knows now, if he did not know it before Japan stabbed our nation in the back at Pearl Harbor, that isolation in this world is an impossibility.

Whether we like it or not, we know that the Divine injunction "No man liveth unto himself alone" applies to nations as well as individuals.

We either must submit or we must fight.

We are fighting not only for our own freedom and our own liberty, but we are fighting for the liberty and the freedom of all the peoples who believe with us that the advancement which the world so far has made in human relationships must be maintained, whatever sacrifice is necessary.

Now, he would address the NAM:

At a recent meeting of the National Association of Manufacturers, the president of that great and powerful organization probably spoke out of turn and exposed the real intention when he said that we are not fighting the war to supply milk for every Hottentot child or to establish a TVA on the Danube.

Any man with a heart and soul, and with vision, can see that, when this war is over, the world must be under the control of men who have no Hitler ideas hidden in their hearts.

This war will be a failure—the peace will be a failure—if we do not provide that, as far as humanly possible, food shall be provided for every innocent babe, regardless of its nationality.

The examples we set here, if truthfully and honestly followed, will result in the establishment of a TVA on the Danube and upon every other river of similar magnitude anywhere in the world.

Norris grew stern: "Men who have spent a lifetime of toil for monopolies and illegal combinations must be freed from the yoke of economic slavery." And his mind was always on public power: "Civilization must get the benefit of the falling water which, when properly controlled, without any loss of substance, and without any interference with its usefulness, will make what we have called, for the want of a better name, 'electricity.' This electricity shall be carried over publicly-owned transmission lines into the homes of our people."

Public development of all resources was his next plea: "Our natural resources must be conserved for the benefit of all the people. These natural resources, God-given, belong to them and must not be owned or controlled by any private monopoly. There must be no place where private monopoly shall make an unholy profit out of the generation and distribution of electricity. The people must all get the benefits and all the joys and pleasures of life these natural resources bring forth."

Norris hammered away: "Yes, we say to the National Association of Manufacturers that the stranglehold which many of its members have had upon the happiness and the destinies of the common man will be loosened and this unseen and mysterious power known as electricity, through the instrumentality of many TVAs, will lessen the labor of those who toil, and will bring happiness, joy, and comfort to every fireside in our land."

What must peace bring? "With hatred toward none, with revenge absent from our hearts, a new world will spread the joys of human life into every home. Monopoly and human greed must be dethroned and, if we are true to the faith, if we are really fighting for freedom, the man who coins the life blood of human toil into money must lose his grip. There will come a time when those who toil, and those who serve, will be placed upon a higher level than those who neither toil nor serve."

Mrs. Roosevelt was on her feet as the program drew to a close. With a broad smile, she presented the senator with a bust of his own likeness sculptured by Jo Davidson.

As tears filled his eyes, and the audience swayed in a mist of sorrow and gratitude, Norris spoke again. He told of the thousands of letters he had received in the past weeks from persons all over the nation, and young servicemen in all parts of the world. "I have not been able to read all of them," Norris whispered. "I cannot see through the tears of gratitude to follow the written page and, in the main, these letters have been read to me by my secretary. In the sunset of my life, when I know I must soon pass over the river, every vestige of sorrow which has entered my heart because of my defeat has been taken away on account of these letters of encouragement."

Thirteen

Out stepped the senator.

By the shrill depot whistle, it was seven o'clock when the front screen door at 706 Main Street swung back into place.

Though bent by time, Norris was right on schedule—as usual. Pausing, the busy-eyed, white-haired man in gray straightened his bow tie, lit a big black cigar, took a deep breath of crisp air, then headed down Main Street to town. His once quick and long steps now were slower and less frequent.

"It's gonna be hot today, Senator Norris," squeaked a breaking voice from across the way. He nodded, spotting the paperboy taking swats at unfortunate flies with undelivered editions.

Crossing the street, Norris met the barber. "'Bout time, isn't it, Senator?" the barber observed with an alert eye on Norris's steel temples. The senator's eyes answered.

On the corner, he paused to sniff a sample of the bakery's early-hour offerings. The aroma of freshly baked pastries was only one of the things that Norris loved about his McCook home.

At the house, Ellie prepared his usual breakfast—two eggs, orange juice, and coffee. Norris made the toast, as always. He spread it with butter; she had orange marmalade.

After breakfast, he read the paper, scanned the mail, then

manned the mower for a trip around the lawn they both kept with pride. For the first time, he felt tired after the abbreviated trip.

Ellie spoke of the spreading weeds in her pansy bed, and Norris disappeared again. He did a thorough job, as she soon would discover.

Lunch brought the senator's favorite dish—chicken and noodles. Up from the table, he moved upstairs to fix the door lock that had sprung loose in the past few days. In minutes, the rap of George William's mending hammer and Ellie's pleading voice were in discord. But he had a mind of his own.

Down again, the lock fixed, Norris settled in his favorite chair off in a corner of the living room. Now, Ellie could relax, too. Stoking his pipe, he leaned forward and grabbed his favorite novel— *Silas Marner*. When Norris was buried in the pages of a good book, he entered the rich world of imagination and left the harsh regrets of stark reality.

Several hours passed before Norris flicked on the radio to catch the late afternoon news. The names of famous Americans with whom he had labored in Washington filled the room. But the name of George Norris no longer was part of the news.

As he twisted the dial, he decided once again—as he had so many times before—that he was going to get one of those new FM sets he had heard so much about.

Now it was time for dinner—liver and lots of mushrooms. And his favorite dessert tonight: apple pie with double thick cream.

While Ellie was in the kitchen, he slipped outside to refurnish the barren pansy patch. Norris was no floral expert.

Back in the house, he slowly climbed the stairs to watch southwest Nebraska's shimmering sunset from a north bedroom window.

His thoughts went back to the fall of 1932.

The sun was just beginning to slide into contact with endless

Nebraska horizon that day as the two men hurried out of town. A pounding echo of hope hammered at their ears as they rode away from the din of a flag-waving multitude.

The stately, open-top Packard rushed them through the still, warm air out to the hill. There, George Norris had something to show his companion. Away from the pressing crowds and the urgent demands of a nation wracked with depression, Norris and his visitor from the East turned to the West.

A shimmering panorama of gold lighted the land. Dispatching warm fingers of yellow across the fields, the fences, and the lonely trees, an outsized sun was aflame as it slipped beyond the edge of the earth. Bathed by the brilliance of the fiery orb, the handsome New Yorker drew inspiration for the final weeks of his headlong dash toward destiny.

Franklin D. Roosevelt always remembered the sunset he saw in the fall of 1932 just west of McCook. He spoke of it often. It was the same sunset that had stirred George Norris so many times as he gazed at it from an upstairs bedroom window in his home or out by the hill.

Dusk was a thing of beauty in the distant green valleys of southwest Nebraska. And for George Norris, it was particularly exhilarating—a source of strength for the many battles in which he had fought. Now, it was a weapon against despair.

Norris sought inspiration elsewhere too—in the tall elm, in Dickens and Shakespeare, along the path of a mile-long walk, and in the martial beat of a band in concert. He found it in the hours he shared with Ellie, in countless conversations with presidents and plumbers, and alone with his cigar.

Ellie knew that it nearly broke his heart that there were not enough trees. That was why the Norris living room walls were crowded with seven pictures of elms and maples and birches. And that was why George William sat in the rocking chair in the corner by the east window, overlooking the park just across the street. There, where he read and dozed in the swan-neck rocker, he could at will catch a glimpse of shade trees.

Norris also worked in the chair, reading, listening, and dictating. In fact, Ellie knew well, he often worked his hardest in his favorite chair.

George William liked his cigars, and Ellie always hated to see him try to quit smoking—as he sometime did. The air was more relaxed when he puffed at a black cigar again.

He had a weakness for Oriental rugs. They were to be found all over the house, four in the east bedroom, where he slept. His favorite red rug lay in the north bedroom, where he watched the sun's daily performance at dusk. Others buried the living room floor and even covered the upstairs hall.

Norris loved books—and they lined shelves in nearly every room. He could be anywhere in the house and not be without a book. Often Ellie and George William read to each other—Shakespeare, poetry, history, biography, works of all the great authors.

He had a fancy for bathrooms. The senator spent a major portion of his younger life without indoor plumbing, Ellie often explained, so he wanted a bathroom for every bedroom in his own home. The house at McCook numbered three bedrooms—and three baths.

Later, Norris was back in the living room where he and Ellie read to each other, awaiting the hour of the band concert in the park. The senator, resting for a moment after a long, full day, felt more tired than he ever had before. Truly, he was growing old, he thought to himself.

Suddenly, it was not easy to rise from his chair. He had to halt now and then to catch his breath. He dreaded the long climb upstairs to his bedroom. He dozed off without warning, and this sometimes annoyed him. He was strangely unsure of himself at times, and even a good night's sleep did not completely rest him. His legs trembled for an instant as he walked down the front steps.

The blaring brass instruments were each groping for the right key when George William and Ellie settled down on the weather-worn benches in the park. Night insects were producing their own concert in the air all around. Then, as darkness came again, the drums began to roll, the brass spoke proudly, and Mrs. Norris cast an affectionate glance at her husband. There were many in the audience who thought it was appropriate.

Under the bright moonlight on the grass in the center of the nation he had served for so long, George Norris listened intently to the strains of "Yankee Doodle Dandy."

Fourteen

Halfway through the five-block trip to the doctor's office, Norris's mind once again flashed back to Washington.

It was spring, and Congress was in session. Senator George Norris was en route by foot to the Senate Office Building from the Dodge Hotel. Washington can be beautiful in the springtime. When it does not rain, the mornings are bright and sunshiny. Such a morning was this. The streets were crowded with early morning traffic. Government workers jammed the sidewalks. A senator could easily become lost in the mob, but Norris was often recognized by strangers, and greetings were exchanged.

The senator had arisen at the usual time, allowing him to be at the breakfast table promptly at seven o'clock He had stepped outside to test the morning air before bidding Ellie goodbye for the day. Then, he was on his way.

At the office, John Robertson had prepared the mail and checked the morning's crowded appointment schedule. He was just beginning to shuffle the senator's late-arriving pile of documents and bills when Norris walked through the door. Robertson cast an eye at the clock. It was, as usual, nine o'clock.

The senator moved quickly to his mail. His full agenda permitted no idle time. Either he must rush through the day's business, or he would fall hopelessly behind. Soon the first visitor would be in the office to keep an appointment set several days earlier. It would continue this way until ten thirty, when Norris must attend a committee meeting.

His visitors were many, and they represented all spheres of the American circle. Some were his colleagues in the Senate, others private citizens with a suggestion, a question, a request, or a gripe. Many more Nebraskans, in the capital sightseeing or on business. Norris saw them all. He chatted amiably about his home state, mutual acquaintances, and Nebraska's interests. He accepted dozens of requests for favors with polite attention. Promising nothing, he then set into motion the machinery that would respond to the wishes of his visitors. Bids for patronage were largely ignored—unless the prospective recipient obviously held the necessary qualifications.

Newsmen came in unusual numbers, and they usually left with a good story, though some came now and then only for background briefing. The Washington press corps relied to a heavy degree on the word of George Norris.

The senator consumed many morning hours during the week in dictation, much of it in response to mail. He always tried to finish by noon. Afternoons were spent in large part away from the office.

When the clock struck noon, Norris was on the floor of the Senate. His absences were rare, and he was habitually punctual. He was never in his office when the Senate was in session. One could not be certain what might suddenly come up on the floor.

Following roll call at noon, Norris would size up the afternoon's debate, choosing the most ideal time for lunch. He ate at the Capitol in a special room frequented by the so-called liberal senators. They usually ate at the same table, enjoying pleasantries in the company of good friends.

Lunch normally came about one o'clock. It lasted twenty minutes or so, sometimes half an hour. A page was always ready to summon the legislators to the floor if the unexpected occurred. The table would include Senators Wheeler, Johnson, Dill, Nye, Cutting, Young Bob La Follette, Howell, and Couzens.

Norris had a private room in the Senate wing, right at the bottom of the stairway leading to the floor. Here, he could work and confer close to the scene. He also had a private office off the Judiciary Committee room in the northwest corner.

The senator remained on the floor (or close to it) until the Senate recessed in the afternoon. Then, it was back to the office for another round of appointments, dictation, and mail. Telephone conferences consumed much time, and before Norris knew it, the clock had passed six.

The senator always tried to get home in time for dinner at seven o'clock. At the Dodge, it was not so difficult. It was when he had lived at the Willard that it had been more difficult. Robertson would drive him to and from work then, and much time was spent in traveling.

The seven to seven schedule persisted with little variance Monday through Saturday. On Sunday afternoon, he would take an auto ride. Robertson drove. Normally they would motor into the country, where Norris could relax and think and plan. The senator enjoyed these trips, and often he would look forward to the beginning of a new week.

Norris could not forget the demanding task of being a senator, even on those excursions out of the capital. He would discuss matters of business with his driver, and together they formulated plans for the week ahead.

The senator paid particular attention to the urgings of Nebraskans, his constituents, his people. They had problems from A to Z. Probably only a senator will ever know how much is expected of a man in his position. Special favors, personal errands, pet projects constantly fill a senator's ears, and he is told to vote every way on every issue. Norris would listen, but he made the decisions.

The senator never wrote letters of recommendation just because he was asked. He had to satisfy himself first that the person in question was able and qualified. Lacking this personal assurance, Norris would not press for his appointment.

He often differed with his colleague from Nebraska, but it made no difference how the other Nebraska senator voted if he voted out of conviction. Personal grudges were not a part of the Norris makeup. Once, he called down a Nebraska congressman for not voting the way he had said he would. It was not the vote that had aroused Norris: it was a lack of honesty or consistency or conviction.

Norris ignored the party line when he cast his own vote on the floor. The party whip did not influence him. He did not shrink from standing in its way. It could snap and crack and whistle through the air, but Norris did not flinch. This independent spirit broke through in 1936 when the split became a gulf. Norris simply did not care what the party position was when he cast his vote. After all, he believed he was elected to represent the people, not his party.

The senator spoke often on the floor. Once he was engaged in a debate that lasted three days, on the issue of a controversial holding company act. Often, he used charts to illustrate his point. Many times, they were the most biting portion of his argument. On the day of a major address, he would receive dozens of requests for copies. But Norris rarely spoke from notes.

The senator knew well that, generally speaking, only those who oppose a bill write concerning its fate. Somehow, those who favor the measure always figure that the preponderance of evidence is so much on their side that additional declarations of support simply are not necessary. So it was that Norris took his mail with a grain of salt, but he still gave it his detailed attention.

Sometimes, Hazel would drop in at the office on her way home. Norris was always pleased, and father and daughter enjoyed their discussion of the day's events.

The storied Huey Long of Louisiana came often. He generally voted on the same side as Norris, and the two men found each other interesting. Long appeared to have a wholesome respect for Norris. The latter considered Long brilliant but often ruthless.

Norris conferred with numbers of senators in the cloakroom, where privacy was assured. Their conferences ranged in subject matter through the entire field of national and international circumstances.

So it was with Senator George Norris. His days in the Senate were full. And there had been many.

He believed he was a United States senator, not just a representative for the people of Nebraska. He believed he must view the problems and hopes of this nation from a national viewpoint, not just from the vantage point of a Nebraskan. Thus it was that he would devote great energy and time to the development of the Tennessee Valley, and this was why he was deeply involved in labor legislation and in amending the Constitution. The interests of Nebraskans could not be divorced from the interests of the nation, he believed.

It was going to be hot today, Norris's perspiring brow forewarned. Yes, the senator smiled, it will be one of those days—one of those days on which he used to douse pressing problems in the cooling waters of the basement Senate swimming pool. Though the pool's waters were refreshing after a long day, the senator still held preference for Wisconsin.

Crossing the senator's path at the east entrance of the Keystone Hotel was the bellhop. He, too, prompted a vivid recollection. Norris thought now of the many times he had chatted with elevator boys at the Senate Office Building. He recalled, too, the three-bell system employed by his colleagues. This assured senators of immediate service to their particular floor by the ringing of the elevator bell three times. Shaking his head, Norris recalled his dislike for the system, which he often considered an imposition upon his visiting constituents. "I'm never in that much of a rush that I cannot wait my turn," he often said. Norris, despite seniority, never pulled rank.

Passing schoolboys refreshed the old-timer's impressions of the page. He was a nice sort of a young man, Norris thought, but oh how he used to get upset over geometry problems. So the senator would occasionally pull the hard-working floor-runner off to one side for explanations of circumference and triangles. With motherly pride, Ellie recalls the afternoon the page whispered to her: "Senator Norris has tutored me through geometry class."

Now, his mind returned to the winter months of 1942, his last weeks in the Senate. The memory of these days was clouded, for these were days of despair, long and lonely, unhappy and distressing.

He had had a large volume of correspondence to answer, much of it sympathetic and kind and heartening. The defeat had unleashed an avalanche of mail. It flooded his office and mounted in stacks that defied all efforts to catch up. Norris and Robertson devoted many hours to dictation. And at last the pile began to dwindle.

As the senator went through the sad, but necessary, motions of closing his office, the Library of Congress began to take an active interest in the historic aspects of the great wealth of material contained therein. The senator's staff had already started to rid the office of some of the bulky files when the library entered the picture with a request. It wanted everything.

Robertson was concerned about what might happen to the file material if it were shipped to Nebraska. The difficulties of transportation were broad enough, but the uncertainty of proper facilities for storage in the home state settled the issue. The files would remain in Washington. The Library of Congress then took over. Its staff moved all the senator's office material—everything from correspondence to souvenirs—to its archives.

That pleased Robertson. Every time an old letter had been torn up in the early days of clearing the office, he had felt a noticeable tug. He just didn't like it. And when library officials gave the order not to destroy anything, he breathed an audible sigh of relief.

So the long and varied history of the days of Senator George Norris was to be preserved for all time. The history of this man was very much the history of the nation itself. It covered a span of forty years' service, two world wars, the Great Depression, and the development of the strongest country in the world. It clearly recorded the awakening of the nation's social conscience and the emergence of its world leadership. Isolation died during those years, and this too was signified in the public career of George Norris. He had voted against U.S. entry into the First World War, and he had opposed American participation in the League of Nations. Now, this same man lent his strength to a war that the United States entered without choice, and he was already planning the peace that would follow with an eye on a cooperative community of nations.

At the library, huge stacks of Norris papers began to form the institution's largest single volume of files. Index cards mounted. It was only with great effort that the collection finally took an orderly form.

Files from McCook, recording the senator's early days in the House, were also moved to the library where the entire collection was assembled for future study.

As Norris mounted the steps to the doctor's office, his mind came back to McCook—and the present. The brief interlude had been pleasant for the senator. Those days on the Hill had been active days, times filled with challenge and duty and dedication. To live them again in retrospect was certainly not like the real thing, but at least it reminded him of the past. And it was the past that held the most joy for George Norris. The present was dull and discouraging. The future was all too certain.

On the second step, Norris paused a moment. That five-block walk had never tired him before. Was it indigestion—or something more? The senator waited for a few brief seconds, then he climbed the remaining stairs.

Walking up to the receptionist's desk, he thought again of Washington and the Senate and the exciting days now gone forever. Yes, the future was all too certain.

Fifteen

"Senator, why were you so bitterly opposed on the TVA?"

Sitting on the grass in back of his home, Norris blew a puff of heavy smoke into the evening air and began to talk. This was one of the moments of the last twenty months that he thoroughly enjoyed—another bull session with soldiers from the McCook Air Base.

They came often; many were regulars and now recognized by name. Others had come this night for the first time. Above them hovered a misty cloud of smoke from their cigarettes and the senator's big cigar.

Boys from the air base began to show up at the Norris door shortly after his return from Washington. They just wanted to see the senator whose name was so familiar and talk with him about the government and the war and the world. Ellie brought them cookies that first visit. And together, Norris and his soldier friends munched pastry and digested the problems of the weary and bloody globe.

Before long, the visits became frequent. Every southern boy whose home was anywhere near the Tennessee Valley began to show up. The backyard was often filled with accents of the Old South. Norris enjoyed that immensely. Far from their homes and those they loved, these homesick boys found a new home with the senator and Ellie. They did not stay long, for they did not wish to tire the senator. And they tried to keep the regularity of their visits reasonable. One thing they could not fully realize—Norris, at home, was also yearning for the world he had left behind. Together, they comforted one another.

One boy from South Carolina used to take the senator for rides in his car. They toured the community Norris knew so well. The senator pointed out spots of interest and acquainted the young southerner with his hometown. The youth, in turn, took Norris to the air base and showed his wartime home to the senator.

As some of his visitors began to know Norris better, they turned from topics of the world to deep personal questions. So a fatherly relationship began to take form. The boys—his boys—would drop in to ask what he would do under the circumstances facing them in settling some burdening personal difficulty. Norris grew increasingly fond of his visitors in khaki. He looked ahead to their next bull session, and eagerly awaited their rap at the door.

The discussions were strictly stag. Ellie didn't join in, mostly because she thought they would prefer that she didn't. But now and then, she would provide the cookies and a refreshing soft drink. Occasionally, a few of the boys were invited to stay for a meal.

The air base meant a great deal economically to McCook. Six thousand men were stationed there, and many of them lived in the town, ate there, entertained themselves there, and bought their clothes, food, and supplies there. Norris had been instrumental in the location of the base. It was fair and accurate to say that the facility very likely would not have been located near McCook if it had not been for Senator Norris.

The senator visited the base many times. It was dusty and desolate and lonely, and Ellie thought every time she saw it what a miserable place it must be to work and live. Norris took an active interest in all that went on about the installation. Sometimes he even used to wonder whether the army knew exactly what it was doing.

The base was the home of B-29 bombers, and the final phase of training for its occupants before they were shipped overseas and from there to the fighting fronts around the torn world.

At the base, Norris asked innumerable questions. He had always been fascinated by planes, and so he enjoyed this close-hand look at America's giant bombers. Sometimes he wished they would offer to take him up with them, but then he knew that the trip might be taxing. At any rate, he was content to examine the craft from top to bottom and discuss its capabilities with any crewman who was handy.

Norris liked to talk about the four big Wright engines, which amassed more than eight thousand horsepower. He liked to sit high in the pilot's seat, viewing the 141-foot wingspan. Norris liked to look up at the twenty-seven-foot-high tail section—which worried him. How could the engines lift such a bulky skeleton of steel? The bomb bays fascinated the visitor too. There, he marveled, was room for more than twenty thousand pounds of bombs.

None of the ten crewmen escaped the inquisitive George Norris. He wanted to know exactly how the bombardier gained his target; how the tail gunner functioned; how the pilot mastered such a craft, and how the navigator plotted such a detailed course. Somehow, Norris could never hear enough about the bombers. And somehow the crewmen could never hear enough from George Norris.

The senator was widely recognized at the installation. Many of his greeters were faces he recognized from the prized sessions at the house. Others introduced themselves and politely inquired as to whether they too might come by sometime for a chat. Norris was pleased.

A fine class of men, the senator told himself. Certainly with this type of fighting man carrying the war to the Axis, victory was assured. But still, how sad and depressing and totally cruel it was to send many of them to their death in some far-off land. Some would find their planes shot out from under them. Others would die from the stuttering fire of an enemy fighter plane. Some would go down with their craft in the midst of German flak. Some would be captured and interred in concentration camps deep in the interior of the enemy's landmass. In the midst of their youth, with so much to live for, they would die.

These thoughts jolted Norris into a new urgency to secure a just peace—one that would endure. Otherwise, what they had given for their country would have been wasted, without lasting benefit to mankind. How Norris wished he could help write that peace.

Often, Norris watched bombers skirting over rooftops in McCook, their engines creating a deafening roar and their giant shadows sweeping across the lawns and streets of his quiet town. Sometimes, they flew so low that the senator considered ducking. But their power and strength never failed to impress him. For a man who had loved to stop and watch planes taking off and landing in Washington, the sight of America's newest weapon of war was inspiring.

Most of the senator's visitors liked FDR. They asked countless questions about the President, and intently listened to personal recollections Norris voiced about his friend in the White House.

Even when the senator did not feel very well, he left orders that any visiting air base soldier be admitted to the home. The visit might be shorter, but it was just as cordial. And, Norris thought, it was good medicine for him, better than that which doctors prescribe.

Norris gave many books to the air base for the enjoyment of

its servicemen. These volumes had been his friends and teachers; now, they could also counsel his boys at the base.

Ellie realized only too well how much the boys at the base were doing for George William. They brought new excitement and inspiration into his life. They gave him a new and valuable outlet, an escape from unhappiness. They provided a compelling interest which made him feel younger again—and happier and healthier. So Ellie was always glad to see a uniform. As one or two or three turned into the gate at their front yard, she smiled and hurried toward the door to greet them. She never failed to notice the flashing gleam in the senator's eyes as the discussion group began its session.

This was also a thrilling moment for the young Georgia boy at the Norris home for the first time. The senator's name had been a symbol to this youth throughout his early manhood. He had read much about Norris and seen his picture dozens of times in newspapers at home. Little had he dreamed that he would one day sit down in the senator's backyard and discuss the problems of the world with him. He had dreaded leaving home to go to war, but like other Americans throughout the nation, he did not shrink from service. Assignment at a base outside a little Nebraska town was not greeted very enthusiastically, and it was only after he had arrived at McCook that he learned that this was the hometown of George Norris, and that he lived there at his home today. The young Georgian often walked the streets of McCook hoping to catch a glimpse of his hero, but he never found him. He walked by the house slowly many times but never saw him. Then, at the base, he met one of the senator's regular visitors, and the meeting was set.

He had now met Norris and sat quietly listening to the conversation. He would write home about it this night. Before he left, he told the senator how much he had admired his long record of public service. He told him how sad he and his family had been to learn of his defeat. He scolded Nebraska, and spoke proudly of the love the South held for Norris. And he did what he had long dreamed of doing as a young man in Georgia. He thanked Senator George Norris for saving the Tennessee Valley, and helping the South.

That night he wrote his parents about the pleasant evening at the Norris home. Having stared at his host throughout the visit, he described him in detail. He repeated the senator's views and a story or two from his experiences in the Senate.

At home, Norris was telling Ellie how he liked the new boy from Georgia and hoped he would come again. Maybe they could invite him to dinner sometime. And so another young man was added to the senator's growing family at the air base.

Little children also came to see the senator. They would spot him out in the yard under a tree or on the sidewalk in front of his home. Running along, talking as they came, they would rush up to Norris to inform him of their newest toy or their plans for the day. This he enjoyed tremendously. Sharing with them the joys of childhood was refreshing. To be recognized by these children was for him far more satisfying than the recognition adults had showered on him for years. All the little folks in the neighborhood seemed to know him—and nothing could have pleased him more.

For the most part they called him "Senator," though some stuck to "Mr. Norris." Others called him "Judge," as had many of their parents since his early days in McCook on the district court bench.

When Norris was not outside, the children would come to the door and ask Ellie if they could see him. Their high, excited chatter filled the house. And nodding, questioning, and agreeing, George Norris listened to the trials and tribulations of a seven-year-old.

Their parents spoke with the senator on the street whenever

they saw him. Often, he surprised them with queries about their son's new baseball bat or their daughter's newest doll. Apologetically, they sometimes asked whether Tom or Joe or Mary had been a nuisance or a bother. But the answer was always the same. No, Norris replied, they were a blessing, not a bother.

The senator also devoted much of his time to the book. The book was a suggestion of many of his close friends. They approached him about it shortly after his defeat, and they applied new pressures throughout the weeks that followed. Some even talked with him about it in St. Louis on the way home. But behind it all, the guiding force was Jim Lawrence.

Lawrence impressed upon Norris the benefit that a chronicle of his life could obtain. Others who would follow might wish to walk with Norris over the long path he followed before they set out on their own. Perhaps his life could light the way as a beacon penetrates the night. Lawrence argued long and hard. In the end, his persuasion prevailed.

Norris dictated in the mornings on his sun porch. In between sittings, he would talk with his stenographer, Ruby Lewis. Norris thought young men should make politics a career, and he often told her so. How could one find a more rewarding, satisfying, or, for that matter, exciting career? And it was a noble career, one of the places in life where a man can do much good for many people.

Dictation started at nine o'clock, and lasted until noon. Norris smoked cigars constantly. Sometimes, while deep in the description of a scene gone by, he paced the floor.

Lewis also helped the senator answer his mail. Even at McCook, it used to come in heavy spurts. One man sent money, expressing the hope that Norris would then be free from financial worries and able to devote his time to thinking. The senator returned the cash with gratitude. Demands poured in for lecture tours and personal appearances, speeches all across the nation and a number of impressive and imposing job offers. Most of the speaking requests were declined; all positions of employment were refused. The replies came largely upon the advice of his doctor, the urgings of Ellie, and the wisdom of his own mind.

Now and then, Norris took a short break to talk with Ellie in the living room or out in the yard. Cigar in hand, he would return refreshed for a new stiff session of dictation. Later, at night, Lewis would return with the typed letters for his signature.

Sometimes, the senator could get angry when he read of developments in Washington over which he no longer had the slightest control. The National Association of Manufacturers often aroused him. The isolationists, critics of U.S. war policy, the profiteers disturbed him. But he vented his anger with reasonable words. They could bite and claw, but they were anchored to reason, not emotion.

Lawrence came to McCook on weekends and together the two friends discussed what had been written and what was to follow. Lawrence edited here and there, with the senator's permission. He checked historical data to be certain dates and events were absolutely accurate. Before long, the book took shape—and the senator had compiled his legacy.

But time was running out.

Sixteen

"Roosevelt is the first president we have had for a long time who is able to look over the top of the Allegheny Mountains," George Norris said.

His visitor from Omaha—a Republican—stiffened without reply.

The senator continued in positive tones: "President Roosevelt has the interests of the entire country at heart. Most presidents have legislated only for the eastern seaboard."

The visitor to the Norris home shook his head. The same old George, he assured himself. He will never change, and I'm not so sure that I would want him to. Regardless of his beliefs, the Omahan contended, Senator George W. Norris is a credit to Nebraska and the entire political system of the United States. But how nice it would have been to have kept Norris openly allied with the Republican Party.

Norris could not have been nicer to his guest and old friend, whom he had not seen for years. The senator showered kind words and hospitality upon the traveler who for so many years had wanted to stop and tell Norris just how he felt about him. But somehow, the appropriate words never came. Norris understood the strength of party convictions, for he too was once like this man. Again, Norris solidified his opposition to unbending party lines.

The visitor was curious about the much-publicized Roosevelt-Norris relationship. The senator found it hard to explain. About all he could tell his old GOP cohort was that they were at ease together. They saw eye to eye on most issues. Disagreement was no basis for discord; rather, it formed the basis for more intent discussion.

The GOP stalwart found it hard to believe when Norris told him that politics was a forgotten issue in the conversations with Roosevelt.

From the kitchen Ellie listened and recalled the senator's associations with the President. Truly, George William and the President had much in common. They still do, she thought to herself, even though they are half a continent apart.

Personal calls from the President had not been uncommon at the senator's office. Roosevelt sometimes phoned several times during a day, especially in the days of the Tennessee Valley's initial legislation. Now, the attentive Ellie told herself: "George William grew where the party didn't."

Every time Norris spoke of his friend in the White House, his tired face reflected a glimmer of hope—a desire to return. Norris wanted to go back to Washington and see Roosevelt and talk with him again, as he had on so many other occasions. Ellie was aware of his intention—and the futility of it.

There had been times when Norris himself had been mentioned as a possible candidate for the presidency. Some midwestern support always developed before the nominating conventions; later, the enthusiasm came more from the South. While it was discussed often, no substantial Norris-for-President drive was ever undertaken. Part of the reason for this was apparently a definite lack of desire on the part of Norris. He never campaigned for the presidential nomination, even to the slightest degree. Norris was content in his seat in the Senate. Whatever was done in the way of booming the senator for a higher political office was done by others.

There was also some talk of nominating Norris for the vice presidency, particularly as a running mate for Herbert Hoover. A definite lack of pleasure was voiced by supporters of Hoover, and the drive never really got off the ground in St. Louis, where Republicans were in convention.

Norris greeted all talk of presidential or vice presidential aspirations with a smile.

The possibility of a presidential appointment to the U.S. Supreme Court was also discussed at times. This Norris probably would have liked—though he never expressed himself publicly on the issue.

The senator's Washington office looked toward the high-domed Capitol. Often, with his feet perched on a table in the Senate Office Building, he would look out the window at the great structure, an architectural source of inspiration.

Sometimes Norris would speak on the floor of the Senate for more than an hour. Ellie watched now and then from the galleries. At home on the night of a particularly lengthy speech, the senator told Ellie his feet ached from the drawn-out session. Then, an eye winking, she would reply: "I wouldn't be surprised if it were your tongue that ached." Norris would laugh.

But he recalled once, it was not only he who was sometimes guilty of talking too long. One day Norris had been on an important speaking tour. He had come into a city by train on a tight schedule that permitted no wasted time. Rushing to the hall where he was scheduled to speak, he walked on stage, sat down and awaited his introduction. Rising to the occasion, the man whose task it was to introduce the senator became lost in his own eloquence. On and on he rambled as Norris nervously watched the clock. When, at last, he came to the conclusion of his opening remarks, Norris rose to say but a quick hello and rush off to his waiting train. So it was not he alone who abused the opportunity of oratory, he reminded Ellie.

Long distance phone bills used to trouble Ellie. Norris cared little how long he talked on the telephone, whether the person he called lived a few blocks away or a thousand miles. And so the bills mounted, and Ellie protested mildly.

The importance of Norris in the life of his nation never seemed to dawn upon him. He considered himself only one of ninety-six senators, but in reality, Norris was a driving force in the newly emerging America. He held influence far beyond that of any other single senator of his time. For he had captured the future before others even saw it. He was a "prophet," as FDR used to say.

He was far ahead of his time, and what he sought he realized only after years of struggle and defeat. Norris went down fighting many times, but on every major issue he rose time and time again before the count of ten, only to finally emerge the victor. Victory came in the late years, and primarily after Roosevelt entered the White House. For Norris, the years of waiting only made the taste of triumph that much sweeter.

In many respects, the senator was the leader of the progressive movement in the United States. His voice reached from coast to coast, from border to border. In every way, he was a national figure.

He would never fully realize how important his service would later be judged. When a national panel of historians, political scientists, and scholars were asked in 1955 to rate U.S. senators for a Senate subcommittee seeking to tab five past members for permanent honors, the panelists named Norris as their top choice. Clay, Webster, Calhoun, all the famous names of the past trailed behind.

Yet Norris remained as controversial after his death as before.

He was stricken from the list approved by the Senate for its Hall of Fame. But politicians don't write the history books.

A man will be judged only by what he accomplishes. What he said does matter, but what he did is the supreme test. Norris could have accomplished little on his own. But it was Norris alone who fought for the liberal cause in its lean years. Year by year, he came closer to accomplishment. To gain it, he needed support. Slowly but steadily it came. So while it was Norris alone who mounted the assault, it was Norris supported and reinforced who won the victory. For shaping much of his country's history, he was chosen by the nation's scholars and historians as the senator most deserving of permanent honor.

Of this, Norris would never know. But those last twenty months at McCook certainly carried the hint. His mail was filled with scholarly inquiries. Editors were still interested. And, now and then, he would hear from some of his colleagues in Washington and even from the president. Stripped of office and power, his influence was not completely gone.

The interest in his biography was gratifying. Sometimes, he would even be asked to comment on the current scene. And his voice was in demand at various points throughout the nation.

The Congressional Library's intense desire to house his records carried a hint. It didn't approach other retiring senators with similar requests, at least to the extent that it was concerned with Norris.

The people of McCook often wondered how the defeat had affected Norris. Apparently not adversely, some thought, because the senator was openly friendly and at no time shunned personal greetings. He must be taking it in his stride, they told one another.

But there were others—his close associates—who thought differently. "George always seems so serious and concerned," the jeweler told the lawyer. The lawyer agreed: "The judge might feel better if he'd let the stream off his chest. It's too bad." The newspaper editor saw the senator as "a man who carries a deep bitterness."

But what did Norris say?

Nothing. He never spoke of the November setback in specific terms. He especially guarded his emotions when talking to his townspeople, who failed to clear the maze of the senator's feelings.

As time grew short, Norris condensed his early morning walks. At first he cut the pace of the journeys, which at times extended more than two or three miles. Then, day by day, the journeys were shortened and eventually abandoned.

The senator's time was now spent in the porch-like study. He read profusely and scanned notes for use in the book. He spent much time on the telephone. Calls were often directed to Lincoln and Jim Lawrence, who was amassing the biography materials. Calls occasionally filtered in from Washington.

When Norris would review the accomplishments of his long life in his own mind, he settled most often upon the REA and TVA. In many ways, they were inseparable. One was an extension of the other. The REA perhaps pleased him most, for it directly benefited his state and his people.

Sometimes, the senator would be criticized for his years of work on behalf of the TVA. Now and then, Nebraskans would ask why such a development had not been not accomplished in his home state instead of far-off Tennessee and its surrounding neighbors. Well, Norris would reply, there was no Muscle Shoals in Nebraska. The TVA, he noted, was a guideline, a beginning that would in the end aid Nebraska in two ways. One would be through the economic benefit to the South. In this nation, what benefits one area is valuable to all the country. The second way in which Nebraskans would share in the TVA's development would be through example. With the proof of the TVA's success came the impetus that would allow public development of other resources in other states.

The REA represented the climax of a dream Norris had entertained throughout his life. Electricity for the farm had been a pet project of the senator's for longer than he could remember. In fact, it had all started when he was a boy on an Ohio farm. As a senator, he pursued the dream. And its realization thrilled him deeply. Perhaps, he thought to himself, this would be his greatest achievement.

His Twentieth Amendment to the Constitution would be of most concern to constitutional historians. The fight to diminish the power of the Speaker of the House would remain alive in the work of students of the legislative processes.

Labor would not forget the anti-injunction law. And certain businessmen, bankers, and financial tycoons were not likely to forget him either.

With these thoughts in mind, Norris wandered into the backyard to join Ellie under the pear tree.

Seventeen

It was a moonlit evening.

Ellie and the senator read to one another under the pear tree. In turn, they shared the writings of Henry Morgenthau. The bright glow of the moon provided all the light they needed. In every way, it was a pleasant August evening.

As the night wore on, they debated whether to remain outside or seek the upholstered comfort of the house. It was the warm and soothing summer evening that prevailed. Reading, talking, and viewing the calm and illuminated night, they sat outside until nearly 10 p.m.

When at last they had come inside, Ellie and Norris went to bed. As they drifted off to sleep, dark clouds began to move toward McCook, dropping rain on dry farmland as they rolled across the Republican Valley.

Later that night, Ellie awoke to the frenzied patter of the falling rain. She arose, walking softly into the hall to close the window. Then Ellie went to George William's bedroom. From the hall, she inquired whether she ought to close his window too. He did not answer. So Ellie crept quietly into the bedroom and shut the window about halfway. George William, she believed, was asleep. But as she returned to the hall, Ellie heard Norris call to her. She stopped. He had said something, but she had not understood. She waited for him to repeat himself, but he did not speak again. He has drifted back to sleep, she thought. Back in bed, Ellie listened for a while to the drops of rain as they clattered on the rooftop. It would be a cool and lovely morning, she decided.

It was the seven o'clock whistle that awakened her. Slipping out of bed, she called to George William: "There's our whistle." It was the usual time to arise.

Norris did not answer. For once, she thought, he is going to oversleep. Ellie began to dress. Then, all of a sudden, without warning, panic struck her. It was not like the senator to sleep past seven. Something was wrong. Ellie rushed to his side. She called, but he did not hear. Her world crumbling about her, Ellie hurried to the telephone.

Doctor Leininger was out of town, so his wife told Ellie she would call Doctor Shank and he would be over immediately. Mrs. George Norris returned to her husband's side. It was, Doctor Shank said, a cerebral hemorrhage. He had apparently been stricken sometime during the night. Members of the family should be summoned. Meanwhile, Doctor Leininger rushed back toward McCook.

It was August 29, a Tuesday. The *Gazette* was filled with the news that American troops were ripping through France toward the German border.

Now the days passed slowly. Norris lay in a semiconscious condition. He was listed as critical. Messages poured in from throughout the nation. The President phoned.

Then, a telegram arrived. "So sorry to hear you are under the weather and I hope much that you will be on your feet again soon," it read. "Affectionate regards. Franklin D. Roosevelt."

Ellie took it to the bedroom. Before she read it to him, Ellie leaned over the bed and spoke softly into George William's ear. "If you understand," she said, "press my fingers." Then, as the wire was repeated aloud, Ellie held her husband's hand. When it was finished, she waited. Suddenly, pressure tightened upon her fingers. Ellie smiled down.

Later, to gain the benefit of a cool breeze, they moved the senator to the east bedroom.

The stroke had been a surprise to Leininger. Norris had seen the doctor regularly every two weeks before his attack, and there had been no hint of any immediate trouble.

The senator remained unconscious most of the time. Paralysis affected his speech. He apparently could hear and seemed to understand what was said to him. But much of the time Norris was beyond comprehension. The doctor called on his patient each morning and evening. Members of his family were always on hand. The President called a couple of times while the doctor was there.

Norris had been Leininger's patient since July of 1943. He had never been fleshy, but he had lost considerable weight in those fifteen months. There had never been any question in the doctor's mind but that Norris was considerably broken up by his defeat, even though he never talked about it. The senator's broken heart might well have had an effect in triggering the stroke, Leininger thought.

Norris had been a good patient. He usually came to the office for his check-ups. The senator was unassuming, but still very impressive, the doctor thought. Norris always dressed well. He was obviously a deep thinker. And sometimes he talked of trees and natural beauty.

Now, he was flat on his back. Flowers filled his room. Ellie was constantly at his side.

The doctor recalled Norris's slight coronary attack in July. He had restricted Norris pretty much after that, for he knew the senator was generally failing. Worry can be hard on a man. It mercilessly drains his strength, and it strains the vital organs of his body. It robs him of sleep, and destroys any opportunity for relaxation. Worry may not have killed George Norris, but it certainly did not help.

The senator's condition worsened to very critical as the first day of September arrived. The *Gazette* told of the pell-mell rush of American troops ever nearer to the enemy border. The end was not far off.

The swan-neck rocker stood empty and motionless. At its side in the glass smoking jar was a handful of big black cigars, each tucked away under cellophane.

The Oriental rugs, for many years a conversation piece, laid unnoticed.

Rows of books, occupying every available shelf, stood intact. Several texts on the sun porch, however, lay open.

The Norris home was silent.

In the Tennessee Valley, great dams gleamed in the late summer sunlight. Farm wives worked under the light of an electric bulb powered by an upstream dam. Water flowed through lush fields, irrigating the soil. There would be no floods this year.

Outside McCook, wires stretched from pole to farmhouse, carrying the energy of public power at low cost to the man who tilled the soil.

On a bloody field on another continent, the next day, the first few American tanks smashed across the border into Germany, the first penetration of enemy soil and the beginning of the end for the Nazi aggressors.

In McCook, the day was clear and warm. The clock in the Norris home stood at 4:25 p.m.

In the east bedroom where his cherished Chinese tables flanked the bed, George William Norris died.

His two bedroom bookcases and the heavy wooden bureau stood against the wall. They still do.

His tobacco jar was half full. It still is.

A giant, beloved tree looked in from the window. It still does.

CPSIA information can be obtained at www.ICGtesting.com
Printed in the USA
BVOW08s1038050913

330315BV00003B/3/P